BELIEVERS

Kingly & Priestly

AUTHORITY

Musa George Mwanza

BELIEVERS KINGLY & PRIESTLY AUTHORITY

E-mail: musagmwanza@gmail.com

ISBN 978-9982-70-552-3

Cover design: The Office 4 u - Jeffreys Bay South Africa.

Table of Contents:

Foreward

These pages you are reading contain powerful tools we need in these last days to take our rightful place in Christ. For He has called us to be Priests and Kings unto Himself in this world. Many children of God have been functioning like tails for far too long, its time to take our Kingship and Priesthood of prayer, to let the light win in you and be the light of your world! Pastor Musa Mwanza in this book reveals the mysteries that have been hidden for ages, this book is a must read for the church, the market place, government officials and for every child of God. This book is a must for every child of God who wants to know his/ her God given right to live a life of kingdom prospective.

Dr. Gershom Sikaala

Author the bestseller title:
You Shall Live, and Break Through Thinking

www.gershomsikaala.org

1

Change of Order

The law and the prophets were UNTIL John: since that time the kingdom of God is preached, and every man presseth into it.

(Luke 16:16).

The Old Testament was based on the law and the prophets as the authority. From the time of Moses to John the Baptist who was the last prophet of the old covenant the law and the prophets reigned. In the old covenant a common believer so to speak had no anointing or authority on him/her. Only the priests, the kings and the prophets would be anointed to stand in their respective offices. A common believer who does not come from the tribe of Judah would not receive kingship. A common believer who does not come from the tribe of Levy would not serve as a priest.

Hence the opening scripture declares that the law and the prophets were until John. Until the time of John the Baptist the old covenant was fully working and the kingdom of God had not yet come. But when the kingdom of God came, the order of things changed. The distribution of authority the priestly or kingly authority was changed. From the time of the Lord Jesus Christ, everyone born in the Kingdom of God has access to the power of the Holy Spirit and the authority of the Word of God. In Christ Jesus are called to royalty, we are called to be joint heirs with the son. The son is the prince of life, the King of kings and the Lord of lords.

> *And if we are (His) children, then we are (His) heirs also: heirs of God and fellow heirs with Christ (sharing His inheritance with Him);*
>
> *(Romans 8:17 AMP).*

We are now God's children and joint-heirs with Christ. The above scripture explains further that to be an heir with Christ is to share in His inheritance. Therefore if all authority in heaven, on earth and under the earth has been given to Christ, then we share in that authority *(Matthew 28:18).* If Christ has been highly exalted and is given a Name that is above all names and at that name every bows and every tongue confesses. We also share the authority and power of the Name. We also are highly exalted together Him. That's what it means to be joint-heirs with Christ; we have a part in everything Christ inherited from the father.

Called to Reign

For if by one man's offence death reigned by one; much more they which receive abundance of grace and of the gift of righteousness shall reign in life by one, Jesus Christ.

(Romans 5:17).

The change of order means that any person male or female, free or slave if they received the abundant grace and the gift of righteousness from our Lord Jesus Christ can reign in this life as a king or priest. You don't have to come from the tribe of Judah to have royal authority neither do you have to come from the tribe of Levy to have priestly authority. In Christ we are called to kingship and priesthood in the Kingdom of God. In Christ we are called to reign in this life with the authority of kings and priests.

And hast made us unto our God kings and priests: and we shall reign on the earth.

(Revelations 5:10).

In this life on earth everyone who has received the grace of our Lord Jesus Christ and the gift of righteousness is made unto God kings and priests. We are bestowed with priestly and kingly authority to reign on this earth. We have power and authority to reign over the kingdom of darkness; the wisdom of the kingdom of darkness and also the wisdom and the kingdoms of this world.

Kingdom of Priests

We are all called to function as kings and priests. This is regardless of what ministry gift the Lord has to given to you. Apostle Paul in his letter to the Ephesians church declared that the Lord has given gifts to men. *"And he gave some, apostles; and some, prophets; and some, evangelists; and some, pastors and teachers." (Ephesians 4:11).* All these men operating in different giftings are primarily called to be kings and priests. We all are a kingdom of priests, a kingdom with Kings and priests reigning with kingly and priestly authority. This also goes to any and everyone who received the grace of our Lord Jesus Christ. Be it Doctors, nurses, school teachers, drivers, servant, slaves, managers, bankers, accountants, engineers, pilots, pastors, etc. Everyone who is born into this kingdom must function either as kings or priests with kingly and priestly authority.

And ye SHALL be unto me a kingdom of priests, and an holy nation. These are the words which thou shalt speak unto the children of Israel.

(Exodus 19:6).

The Lord was speaking in the future when He told the children of Israel that they shall be a kingdom of priests in the scripture above. He was speaking into the new order. He didn't mean to say that every one of the children of Israel shall be a Levite, but He said this looking at the time when His Kingdom has fully come on earth. The Lord used the word shall as capitalized in the above scripture to mean that, this will not happen now but in the future when the kingdom of God has descended. This Word was for the church, the one new man, the new creation and is still for the new covenant church. The Spirit through apostle Peter confirmed this in the scripture below:

But ye ARE a chosen generation, a royal priesthood, an holy nation, a peculiar people; that ye should shew forth the praises of him who hath called you out of darkness into his marvellous light.

(1Peter 2:9).

Peter the apostle wrote on the fulfillment of the promise God the father made to the church. In exodus the Lord said *"you **shall** be unto me a kingdom of priests and a holy nation……..."*But in 1ˢᵗ Peter the same Lord spoke through Apostle Peter saying ***"you are a chosen generation, a royal priesthood, a holy nation..."***

9

We are a kingdom of priests, a chosen generation, royal (kingly) priesthood, a holy nation a peculiar (mysterious) people called and given authority to show forth praises of Him who has called us out of darkness into His marvelous reigning light. All of us have this authority to show forth His praises. We all have it whether pastor or usher; whether bishop or sweeper we all are called into this glorious royal priesthood. We all have the authority to be kings and priests and to reign in this life through Christ Jesus our Lord.

Moses and Elijah

Moses and Elijah are the two examples of how the Lord wants want the new creation to function. He has given us these two as our example of how kingly and priestly authority works. Elijah was a prophet but he reigned on earth as a Priest. His ministry on earth was highly priestly. He was not born in the order of priesthood but the Lord prepared him as an example of a royal priest to the church *(2 Kings 17:1).* Moses on the other hand is the example of Kingly authority. Moses like Elijah did not have kingly order in him but the Lord prepared him to be the example of kingly authority to the church.

These two men lived in different times but the Lord used each of them differently to introduce a different order of doing things. Both these men walked very close to God and understood the secrets of divine power and authority respectively. Finally the Lord honoured both these men by not allowing their bodies to be buried on earth. Elijah went to heaven without seeing death and Moses' body was taken by Archangel Michael *(Jude 9)*, And buried in the valley of Moab by the Lord Himself *(Deuteronomy 34: 6).*

The official closing Words of the Lord God in the old covenant as recorded in the last chapter of the book of Malachi were as follows; remember the law of Moses and I will send you Elijah before the great and dreadful day of the Lord. These Words marked the official end of an era, but were the secret behind the order of things in the new covenant.

> *"Remember ye the law of Moses my servant, which I commanded unto him in Horeb for all Israel, with the statutes and judgments. Behold, I will send you Elijah the prophet before the coming of the great and dreadful day of the LORD."*
>
> *(Malachi 4:4-5).*

The kingly and priestly authority which these giants operated in pleased the Lord that He saw it fit for the new covenant church to emulate. These two giants of the faith did wonders using the power and the authority of God. They showed us how we ought to operate in this kingdom. They showed us how we ought to reign in this life with the kingly and priestly authority in Christ Jesus.

Moses' kingly authority overcame the great kingdom of Egypt. Moses' authority was in the "rod," as is recorded in the book of Exodus 4:17; ***"And take in your hand this rod with which you will do the signs (BBE)."*** With the same rod he led his people in the desert for 40years, did numerous signs and wonders and subdued kingdoms. Moses with the authority judged his people with righteousness. He fellowshipped with God as a friend as kings do. He healed all that were sick in the camp by the Kingly authority given to him by God most high. He wiped out his adversaries and received the commandments firsthand from God. Moses was made as "God" to pharaoh the King of Egypt. ***"The Lord said to Moses, behold, I make you as God to pharaoh (to declare my will and purpose to him)......."*** ***(Exodus 7:1 AMP).*** Moses received kingly authority to function like God towards pharaoh. He was a form of Christ, a form of an emblem of the coming King.

> "For Moses truly said unto the fathers, A prophet shall the Lord your God raise up unto you of your brethren, LIKE UNTO ME; him shall ye hear in all things whatsoever he shall say unto you."
>
> (Acts 3:22).

The scripture above talks about Christ Jesus being that prophet that Moses talked about. This scripture was actually a confirmation of what Moses prophesied in the old about a prophet who is Jesus Christ our Lord.

Elijah on the other hand was a symbol of the priestly authority. He operated with the "mantle" which is the symbol of the priestly authority, the power of the Holy Spirit. Elijah with his priestly authority went to heaven without ever seeing death *(2 Kings 2:11).* He raised the dead, was divinely transported from one location to another supernaturally *(1 Kings 17:22; 1 Kings 18:12).* He destroyed the 400 false prophets; the prophets of Baal *(1 Kings 18:40).* He called fire from heaven to consume the sacrifice (1 Kings 18:38). He provided for the widow food supernaturally (1 Kings 17:16). He prayed that it should not rain in the land of Israel and it did not rain for three and half years. He prayed again that it should rain and it did rain. *"Elias was a man subject to like passions as we are, and he prayed earnestly that it might not rain: and it rained not on the earth by the space of three years and six months. And he prayed again, and the heaven gave rain, and the earth brought forth her fruit." (James 5:17).*

He outran the chariots of horses *(1 Kings 18:46),* and destroyed armies. Elijah called fire from heaven to destroy his adversaries *(2 Kings 1:10-13).* Above all he had disciples and raised a prophet who functioned in the same priestly authority as he did. Elijah functioned in the power that the Lord intended for the new creation in Christ to function in. He is an example of how much we can function with the priestly authority.

These two examples of power and authority are the way the Lord intended for us to function. We are called to function in the anointing and power of Moses as kings and also in the anointing and power of Elijah as priests. The fact that Moses and Elijah appear again in the New Testament on the Mount of Transfiguration and again in the book of Revelations confirms this. *(See Matthew 17:11; Revelations 11:1-14).* Moses and Elijah are powerful examples of how God wants to continue to operate with His people.

Partakers in the Godlife

I am the vine, ye are the branches: He that abideth in me, and I in him, the same bringeth forth much fruit: for without me ye can do nothing.

(John 15:5).

We are called to live the very life that the Godhead has. This is the life that we receive when we are born again. This Godlife is what is called eternal life. *"Verily, verily, I say unto you, He that believeth on me hath everlasting life." (John 6:47).* Everlasting life living in us and us living in the everlasting life in Christ makes us partakers of the Godlife. Having the Godlife living in us makes us share in the authority of the Godlife. The essence of the Godlife is in its supremacy over human life, animal life and plant life. It is the very life of God. This life we received from Christ, the life eternal and full of power and authority.

> *"I have said, Ye are gods; and all of you are children of the most High."*
>
> *(Psalms 82:6).*

The psalmist said of God as a judge who judges in the assembly of gods. One may think that God meant some heavenly beings when He said He judges in the congregation of the gods. The same scripture but verse 6 as shown in the above quoted scripture shows us that the gods he meant was us. It shows that God meant the new creation, born again believers. You and I are gods. You and I children of the most high God. The lord Jesus confirmed this in ***John 10:35***; when he said ***"If he called them gods, unto whom the word of God came, and the scripture cannot be broken." (John 10:35).*** The scripture cannot be broken. The men who received the scripture are called gods by the Most High God because they became partakers of the Godlife. The Lord Jesus quoted and confirmed what the psalmist wrote of God. You and I, and the rest of the believers are the ones to whom the Word of God came. You and I are therefore called gods because we have the life of God in us.

We are called to reign in this life. We are called to be the light and the salt in this world. This life that we are made to partake comes with the authority and power of the Godhead. *"For it is impossible for those who were once enlightened, and have tasted of the heavenly gift, and were made partakers of the Holy Ghost, and have tasted the good word of God, and the powers of the world to come." (Hebrews 6:4-5).*

The Godlife brings enlightenment, gives us the authority to use the heavenly gifts, makes us partakers of the Holy Ghost and experience the goodness of the Word of God and finally we are given the powers of the heavenly. This life brings us to the place where we function as Kings, Priests and Lords. In the Old Testament we are given a few examples of the people who functioned with authority as kings and Priest. These people used their authority to save nations, to become the best, reveal deep and hidden secrets and overcome odds. Moses commanded the red sea and it gave way for the children of Israel to cross on dry ground. *"And the LORD said unto Moses, Wherefore criest thou unto me? Speak unto the children of Israel, that they go forward: But lift thou up thy rod, and stretch out thine hand over the sea, and DIVIDE IT: and the children of Israel shall go on dry ground through the midst of the sea." (Exodus 14:15-16).*

The Lord God did not divide the sea for Moses and the children of Israel. He asked Moses: *"Why are you crying to me?"* This is because He knew that Moses had the Godly authority and power of the Godlife to divide the red sea. The Lord then told

Moses how to use his authority to divide the sea. The same happens with us, the Lord will not exercise your authority for you. He gives you the authority for you to use.

Elijah commanded the sky not to give rain in the land of Israel until at his word and the sky got shut. *"And Elijah the Tishbite, who was of the inhabitants of Gilead, said unto Ahab, As the LORD God of Israel liveth, before whom I stand, there shall not be dew nor rain these years, but according to my word." (1King 17:1).* Elijah the Tishbite, boldly said until at my word it will not rain in this land. This is very outstanding; this man knew the authority he had in his word. He didn't say until the Lord say so. He said according to my word. This is because Elijah understood the priestly and Kingly authority he had. This man understood that this authority was given to sons of men. He understood the fact that God had made him like a God to this world. He understood that man in his original state has dominion over all the created things *(Psalms 8:6).*

Like Elijah the Tishbite, there were other men who understood the authority God had given them. We have Joshua who commanded the sun to stop and it stopped. *"Then spake Joshua to the LORD in the day when the LORD delivered up the Amorites before the children of Israel, and he said in the sight of Israel, Sun, stand thou still upon Gibeon; and thou, Moon, in the valley of Ajalon. And the sun stood still, and the moon stayed, until the people had avenged themselves upon their enemies. Is not this written in the*

book of Jasher? So the sun stood still in the midst of heaven, and hasted not to go down about a whole day." *(Joshua 10:12-13).*

In a manner similar to Moses, Elijah and even our Lord Jesus, Joshua commanded the sun to stop. Notice that he didn't ask God to stop the sun on his behalf but he commanded the sun to stop and It stopped. He spoke to the sun and commanded the sun to stop at Gibeon and to the moon and commanded it to stop in the valley of Ajalon. Joshua simply exercised his authority as a king and priest over all the creation. The account of this event is recorded in the scripture as shown below:

"Then spake Joshua to the LORD in the day when the LORD delivered up the Amorites before the children of Israel, and he said in the sight of Israel, Sun, stand thou still upon Gibeon; and thou, Moon, in the valley of Ajalon. And the sun stood still, and the moon stayed, until the people had avenged themselves upon their enemies. Is not this written in the book of Jasher? So the sun stood still in the midst of heaven, and hasted not to go down about a whole day."
(Joshua 10:12-13).

Elisha commanded metal to float on water and it floated. Elisha like the other sons of men who walked close with God also did not ask the Lord to float the iron head of an axe. He simply picked a stick and used it as a contact point to exercise the authority given from God to make the iron axe head float. Elisha did not kneel down and start praying asking God to bring the axe head back; he simply used his authority to make it float. *But as one was felling a beam, the axe head fell into the water; and he cried, and said, Alas, my master! for it was borrowed. The man of God asked, "Where did it fall?" He showed him the place. He cut down a stick, threw it in there, and made the iron float. He said, "Take it." So he put out his hand and took it. (2Kings 6:5-7 WEB).*

Prophet Daniel and his companions had 10 times more wisdom and understanding than the peers of his day. They were found to be more wise and understanding than all the magicians, astrologers and wise men of the day. *"In every matter of wisdom and understanding, concerning which the king inquired of them, he found them ten times better than all the magicians and enchanters who were in all his realm." (Daniel 1:20).* Many more guys both in the Old and New Testament defied the odds with the authority and power of the Godlife.

Jesus the First Royal Priest

The Lord Jesus is our perfect example of a king and a priest. He is the first in the form of how God the father wanted us to operate. The lord Jesus was born from the genealogy of the tribe of Judah. This lineage of the tribe of Judah was kingly lineage. He was also known as the son of David who makes Him royalty. *"The book of the generation of Jesus Christ, the son of David, the son of Abraham." (Mathew 1:1).* He was born as a king in the line of David his father.

The Lord Jesus was also a priest. But because He was born from the tribe of Judah He could not be a priest in the line of Aaron the Levite. His priestly hood is of another order. At the time of the birth of our Lord Jesus Christ, Zachariah the father of John the Baptist was the Priest. Zachariah had a son named John who was of priestly descend and therefore was a priest by birth. John the Baptist came in the Spirit and anointing (Dunamis) of Elijah *(Luke 1:17).* And he went about doing his priestly duties of preaching repentance and that the kingdom of Heaven is at hand. *"And saying, Repent ye: for the kingdom of heaven is at hand." (Mathew 3:2).*

John in order to fulfill righteousness had to baptize Jesus into his office. The same priestly office John the baptized had *(Mathew 3:15).* John the baptized gave out his priestly authority to Jesus at the time of baptism. This is because Jesus was not eligible for priesthood by virtue of Him being born from the tribe of Judah. Therefore when John who was a priest gave out his priestly anointing to Jesus, his ministry ended. *"Now after that John was put in prison, Jesus came into Galilee, preaching the gospel of the kingdom of God." (Mark 1:14).* This was immediately after baptizing Jesus that he (John the baptized) was put in prison. This was because John had finished his assignment of preparing the priestly way for the Lord on earth. Hence John's saying I must decrease so that Jesus must increase. *"He must increase, but I must decrease." (John 3:30).*

The Lord started to do the same things John the baptized was doing and preaching the same massage John was preaching. **"From that time Jesus began to preach, and to say, Repent: for the kingdom of heaven is at hand." (Mathew 4:17).** The Lord Jesus ministered as a priest under the same spirit and power (Dunamis) as Prophet Elijah the same way John the baptized preached the Kingdom of Heaven.

The Lord Jesus therefore operated as a king with kingly authority and also as a priest, with priestly authority. He took the operation and workings of Moses as a king and the operations and working of Elijah as a priest. Remember when Jesus was ministering on earth He did not minister as the son of God. He ministered as the son of man. The same way you and I operate here on earth. Elijah operated as a man of passions like us here on earth *(James 5:17).* Moses too was a man like us here on earth (exodus 3:11).

Therefore Jesus ministered on earth in the same manner as Moses and Elijah did. Jesus could not bring or operate as a son of God here on earth because it would mean that He wouldn't bc tempted like us. *(Hebrews 4:15).* This would therefore mean that Jesus would have been in a class of His own unreachable by anyone operating on earth as a son of man. But Jesus Himself said; these things I do you shall do also, even greater things shall you do because I am going the father.

> *"Verily, verily, I say unto you, He that believeth on me, the works that I do shall he do also; and greater works than these shall he do; because I go unto my Father."*
>
> *(John 14:12).*

Jesus operated like one of us when He ministered here on earth. When He asked His disciples who people say that He the Jesus (the son of man) is? Many said He is john the Baptist, Elijah or one of the prophets of old. This is because they could see the similarities in operations between Jesus and Elijah or John the Baptist who moved in the spirit and power of Elijah.

> *"When Jesus came into the coasts of Caesarea Philippi, he asked his disciples, saying, Whom do men say that I the Son of man am? And they said, Some say that thou art John the Baptist: some, Elias; and others, Jeremias, or one of the prophets."*
>
> *(Mt 16:13-14).*

Many in those days thought one of the prophets has arisen or even john the Baptist. This was Jesus ministering in the same authority as Prophet Elijah.

Moses on the other hand declared that the Lord will raise a prophet like him whom they should listen to. Moses meant Jesus when he said these words. He knew that the day will come when this prophet will deliver the people for the bondage of sin. The same way he delivered the children of Israel from the bondage of slavery.

> *This is that Moses, which said unto the children of Israel, A prophet shall the Lord your God raise up unto you of your brethren, LIKE UNTO ME; him shall ye hear.*
>
> (Acts 7:37).

Jesus was that prophet like unto Moses in His operations. He is the King and judge over Israel like Moses was. Moses gave the children of Israel manna from heaven and Jesus gave the church (Jews and Gentiles in Him) the bread of life.

Jesus moved with authority and with power in His earth ministry. The same authority and power God intended for us to operate in. Jesus' words were full of authority and power. He spoke with authority and surety the same way Elijah told King Ahab that until at my word, it shall not rain in the land of Israel.

"And they were all amazed, and spake among themselves, saying, What a word is this! for with authority and power he commandeth the unclean spirits, and they come out."

(Luke 4:36).

Jesus moved in this authority as a king and a priest. He is the first born of all the royal priests, the kingly priests. You and I are born with the same privilege of being royal priests like Jesus. Jesus is the King over you and I the kings. That's why He is called king of kings. He's king over us kings. ***"These shall make war with the Lamb, and the Lamb shall overcome them: for he is Lord of lords, and King of kings: and they that are with him are called, and chosen, and faithful." (Revelations 17:14).***

He is also the High Priest. Jesus is the High priest over us the priest. ***"Wherefore, holy brethren, partakers of the heavenly calling, consider the Apostle and High Priest of our profession, Christ Jesus." (Hebrews 3:1).*** He is our high priest who ever live to perform priestly duties for us interceding for us.

Let us take up our place of royalty and reign in this life. The Psalmist said they do not know nor do they understand. ***"They know not, neither will they understand; they walk on in darkness: all the foundations of the earth are out of course. I have said, Ye are gods; and all of you are children of the most*** *high. But ye shall die like men, and fall like one of the princes."(Psalms 82:5-7).*

The Lord has made us like Gods in this world, that same way; He made Moses like God to pharaoh. The foundations of the earth are out of course because like mere men, without power and authority to uphold all things in their respective places and order. With the priestly and kingly authority received from our lord Jesus we have power to uphold all things in their original places and order **(Hebrews 1:3).**

The Words in the highlighted scripture above are yours to ponder. You choose! Die like a mere man when God made you like Him with authority and power? Or rise up! Get knowledge and live like a king and a priest that you are?

The following chapters of this book will explain to you more about the authority and power of Kings and Priests. Go on, study on, get knowledge and restore the foundations of the earth.

2

Authority and Power

"And they were all amazed, and spake among themselves, saying, What a WORD is this! For with AUTHORITY and POWER he commandeth the unclean spirits, and they come out."

(Luke 4:36).

Many in the days of our Lord Jesus were used to the teachings of the Pharisees which was full of ideologies and empty doctrines. But when the Lord Jesus appeared on the seen, he brought about a teaching which had authority. He taught in the synagogues with authority. *They were amazed at his teaching, because his message had authority,"* *(Luke 6:32 NIV).*

He used his authority even when dealing with the evil spirits. He commanded them with authority and charged them to leave the victim at once and they obeyed and left each time. **"Be quiet!"** *Jesus said sternly "come out of him!" Then the demon threw* *the man down before them all and came out without injuring him." (Luke 4:35 NIV).*

The other incidence the Lord Jesus displayed power over sickness. In this incidence, the scripture did not say that Peter's mother-in-law had evil spirits, but she had a fever. A fever can be caused by any sickness that can naturally occur. The Lord Jesus used the power in his word to dispel that sickness the same way he used the authority in his word to drive out demon spirits. *"Jesus left the synagogue and went to the home of Simon. Now Simon's mother-in-law was suffering from a high fever, and they asked Jesus to help her. So he `bent over her and rebuked the fever, and pt left her. She got up at once and began to wait on them." (Luke 4:38-39 NIV).*

The power and authority of God the Lord Jesus used is released through the Word. The scripture above shows how the people were amazed at the power and authority that was released in the word spoken by the Lord Jesus during his earthly ministry. With the authority of the word he commanded evil spirits and they obeyed and left, with the power in the word he rebuked the fever that Peter's mother-in-law had and it left at once.

Authority

The Word AUTHORITY as used in the opening scripture comes from a Greek root word EXOUSIA. This Word exousia is used to mean delegated authority, mastery or superhuman authority. The Greek word exousia comes from a primitive Word exousiazo. This Word exousiazo means *"to have control: exercise authority upon."* It also means to *"bring under the power of."* The Word-delegated authority refers to acting on behalf of the other. In this vein it means acting on behalf of the Lord Jesus, using the divine authority of God.

This superhuman or divine authority has been given to us for to operate with here on earth. This authority comes straight from on high for us who have been called according to His purposes. This authority has been given to help us thwart the powers of darkness; it is also given to help us overcome the authority and the wisdom of this world.

"For whatsoever is born of God overcometh the world: this is the victory that overcometh the world, even our faith."

(1 John 5:4).

The Word used to mean overcome is a Greek word, which also means to subdue or to get victory over; with this authority we can subdue and get victory over the wisdom and the kingdoms of the world.

This delegated authority is given to us through the Word of God. This authority is found in the word of God; it comes from the word of God. This is shown in the scriptures below:

> *"For he taught them as one with authority (exousia), and not as the scribes."*
>
> *(Mathew 7:29).*

The Word at work in your life will produce the divine authority of God in you. This is the authority that we use to overcome the powers of the enemy.

Power

> *"And they were astonished at his doctrine: for his word was with Power (Exousia)."*
>
> *(Luke 4:32).*

The Word POWER as used in the opening scripture above comes from a Greek Word DUNAMIS. The Word Dunamis is used to mean miraculous powers, mighty wonderful work, and ability to do mighty deeds. The Word Dunamis comes from a Greek primitive word Dunamai. This Word "Dunamai" means, *"to be able"* or to *"be of power."* This means that if you have the Dunamis working in you; you have power to do the miraculous, power to perform miracles, Power to be witnesses for Christ through doing the might wonderful works. The Word "Dunamai" also shows us that we are well able to do the impossible with dunamis working in our lives.

The power to do the miraculous is found in the Holy Spirit. It is packaged as a seed of power given to everyone who has received the Holy Spirit as shown in the scriptures below:

"And, behold, I send the promise of my father upon you: but tarry ye in the city of Jerusalem, until ye be ENDUED with POWER(Dunamis) from on high."

(Luke 24:49).

The Word <u>endued</u> as highlighted in the scripture above comes from a Greek word **"enduo."** Enduo means to sink into a garment, to invest and or to put on. This implies that as the Spirit comes upon us, he baptizes us with power, the Spirit sinks us in power. The Spirit also invests seeds of the miraculous in us giving us the enablement or the ability to do the supernatural.

"But ye shall receive POWER (Dunamis), after that the Holy Ghost is come upon you: and yet shall be witnesses unto me..."

(Acts 1:8).

Dunamis gives us the ability to know and experience Jesus. The Spirit through Dunamis makes us witnesses to the death and resurrection of Jesus. A witness is that who has seen with his eyes and know exactly what happened. For this reason the Holy Spirit through the Dunamis makes us see the reality of what Jesus did for mankind on the cross and what he accomplished thereafter. This is why when the Holy Spirit comes upon us, he makes us to witness with boldness and confidence because our spirits and hearts are made to see and understand the significance of what Jesus accomplished for us. That is why the Lord Jesus said to Nicodemus; *"I tell you the truth, we speak of what we know, and we testify to what we have seen, but still you people do not accept our testimony." (John 3:11 NIV)*.

Notice that the Lord Jesus did not say **"I"** speak of what I know, but instead He said; **"WE"** speak of what we know and testify to what **"WE"** have seen. This shows that He did not only speak for Himself but for others as well. This is to symbolize that anyone who has the Spirit and the Dunamis working in him is a part of the "we". This is because whoever has the Dunamis working in him will be made a witness also by the working of the Holy Spirit in him through the Dunamis. He will be made to know (perceive, understand) and see by the Holy Spirit so that he can be a witness to the glory to God!

3

Kingdom of God and Kingdom of Heaven

A kingdom is a domain that is ruled by the King. Every kingdom has rulership. The scriptures declare in many instances that the Kingdom of God and the Kingdom of Heaven has come. The Lord Jesus when he showed his disciples how to pray in *Mathew 6:10* showed us of the existence of two kingdoms and commanded us to pray and ask for both the kingdoms to come. He said; *"Thy Kingdom come." "Thy will be done in earth, as it is in heaven."* The words "<u>will</u>" and "<u>kingdom</u>" means the same thing; in a kingdom the will of the king is law. The scriptures, Bible directly translated from Hebrew to English puts it this way; *"let your reign come, let your desires be done on earth as it is in heaven."* In place of Kingdom, the scriptures use the word *REIGN,* in place of will it uses *DESIRE*. The sovereignty of God demands that His desires in heaven govern the heavens. This is the same that Christ commended us to ask from the Father, for His desires to be carried out on earth as it is in heaven.

This then means that He commended us to pray for the Kingdom of God and the Kingdom of heaven to come and manifest in our lives, for His reign and His desires in heaven to manifest in our lives and ministries. *"Thy Kingdom come"*---the Kingdom of God; *"Thy will be done in earth as it is in heaven"*---the Kingdom of heaven.

These Kingdoms live in us and we live in them at the same time. Similarly Christ lives in us and we live in Christ. So then, if a kingdom is about rulership then the Kingdoms of God and Heaven in us are some form of authority in our lives. These two Kingdoms have two distinct roles in our lives. They provide us with two different tools we need for our everyday victories over the world and the devil.

The Kingdom of God

"...Jesus came into Galilee, preaching the GOSPEL of the KINGDOM OF GOD."
(Mark 1:14).

The word used for Kingdom is a Greek word **"Basileia."** This word basileia means to rule or reign. The scripture above therefore entails that the Lord Jesus went throughout Galilee preaching the goodnews of the reign of God. The rule of God was the main reason for the coming of the Lord Jesus on earth. God wanted to restore His rule back on earth, just like it was in Eden. In the Garden of Eden there was a perfect communion between God and man, which allowed man to execute the rule of God on earth on God's behalf. Man became the official ambassador and executor of the rule of God on earth. This is found in the first book of the Bible. In the book of Genesis God gave man this rule to man to execute on His before as shown below;

And God blessed them, and God said unto them, Be fruitful, and multiply, and replenish the earth, and SUBDUE IT: and have DOMINION over the fish of the sea, and over the fowl of the air, and over every living thing that moveth upon the earth.

(Genesis 1:28).

The command to rule on God's behalf is found in the word SUBDUE IT. The word subdue comes from a Hebrew word "Kabash," which means to bring into subjection. This gives us the authority to bring every power, dominions, situation and circumstance into subjection to the rule of God. The second command given was the authority to rule on God's behalf over every created thing on earth. This command is given in the word DOMINION, which comes from a Hebrew word "Radah,"which means to reign or to rule.

The Kingdom of God was given, for us to rule the earth, with the delegated authority living in us.

This kingdom has its authority hidden in the word of God. This therefore means that the more the word of God is working in you the more the Kingdom or rulership of God is working in you. This Kingdom was given to us for the purposes of overcoming the rulers and kingdoms of the world, it is the authority given, for us to overcome the world.

"For whatsoever is born of God overcometh the world: and this is the victory that overcometh the world, even our faith."

(1John 5:4).

Our victory over the world is our faith in the Word of the King. The more we believe the Word of the King and put it to work in our lives the more royalty we become. The authority in the Kingdom of God is EXOUSIA, and this authority is found in the Word of God. He, who has the Word in him, has the Kingdom in him and he who has become one with the Word in him, through meditation has the KING in him.

"In the beginning was the Word and the Word was with God and the WORD WAS GOD."

(John 1:1).

"And he was clothed with a vesture and dipped in blood: his name is called The WORD OF GOD."

(Revelations 19:13).

The first scripture shows us that God is one with His Word. The second one shows us that Jesus is called the Word of God. So if the Word has become alive in you, you become a King, because you and His Word which is Him have become one.

In the Kingdom of God we exercise authority in the Name of Jesus. The Kingdom of God gives us Authority over things on earth, things in heaven and things under the earth. The Name of JESUS is a doorway to access the authority in the Kingdom of God. This is the Authority we have over all the powers of the enemy.

"That at the name of Jesus every knee should bow, of things in heaven, and things in earth, and things under the earth."

(Philippians 2:10).

The Name JESUS is the doorway to power and authority in the Kingdom of God. The scripture above declares that every knee bows at the authority accessed in the Name of Jesus. Every knee in the ranks in heaven, in the ranks on earth and in hell bows at the Exousia, the authority in the rule of God. This is the Authority we are given to function in, the authority to affect heaven, earth and hell in the Name of Jesus. It's your set time to reign as a King with the exousia. In the Kingdom of God we exercise authority by FAITH. Glory to God!!!

Faith is a leap onto the Word of God; it is not going into the unknown, it is not an emotion. It is a step onto the promises of God in his Word. To exercise authority by faith means to exercise the authority of the Word of God in faith. Faith is not based on the confidence we have in the men of God, it is not about acting on what we what we have seen and heard, but on the Word of God. The authority in the Word of God is what overcomes the world, it is this authority used in faith that overcomes the Kingdom of darkness. You cannot have faith if you don't first believe the Word of God. One has to have a genuine trust in the Word of God in order to have faith and exercise the authority of God in His Word. Complete trust in the Word of God is the preliquisite for exercising the authority given in faith to act on God's behalf.

Misunderstanding Authority

The scripture in *(Acts 19:13-16 NKJV)* as shown below gives us a classic example of the effects of lack of proper understanding of Authority;

"Then some of the itinerant Jews, exorcists, took it upon themselves to call the name of the Lord Jesus over those who had the evil spirits, saying, "We exorcise you by the Jesus whom Paul preaches." Also there were seven sons of one sceva, a Jewish chief priest, who did so. And the evil spirit answered and said,

"Jesus I know, and Paul I know, who are you?" Then the man in whom the evil spirit was leaped on them, and overpowered them, and prevailed against them, so that they fled out of that house naked and wounded."

The sons of sceva were children of a High Priest, the Chief High Priest for that matter. This meant that these children grew up in the house of the Lord; they are sons who grew up seeing and hearing about the authority and power of the Word of God. Now these sons went out casting out demons, the same way Paul did. However they did not understand the authority and power of the Name of Jesus, which Paul used. The kingdom of darkness recognizes the authority in the kingdom of God, that's why the evil spirits did not recognize the authority with which the sons of sceva were using. The evil spirit answers and said, "The authority of Jesus I know?" "The authority of Paul I know?" "But whose authority are you using?" This now shows that faith should always be based on the Word and authority of God and not on what you've heard and seen. The kingdom of darkness in this case overcame these men even though they were using the Name of Jesus. This is because these men did not have the authority of the kingdom of God; they did not have the exousia, the authority of the Word of God. This therefore means that faith is only faith when you leap on the Word of God with the understanding of the authority of the Word of God.

The Kingdom of Heaven

"From that time Jesus began to preach, and to say, Repent: for the Kingdom of heaven is at hand."

(Mathew 4:17).

The word used for Heaven is a Greek word, which means the abode of God. By implication it represents happiness, power and eternity. The coming of the Kingdom of Heaven on earth brings the will of God in Heaven to earth. *Mathew 6:10* show us that the Kingdom of Heaven brings Heaven on earth. By implication this means that the Kingdom of Heaven brings happiness, POWER and eternity. The word power as highlighted above comes from a Greek word DUNAMIS. This then means that the power that comes from the Kingdom of Heaven is the miraculous power, the power that comes from the Holy Spirit. The meaning of the Greek word used for Heaven in the above scripture is the abode for God. This word also means a tabernacle or a temple. The coming of the Kingdom of Heaven brought the reality of Heaven to earth. The coming of the Holy Spirit brought about this Kingdom. By the Holy Spirit God the Father dwells with us, by the same Spirit we are his people and by the same Spirit He brings the reality of heaven in our lives and ministries.

"And I heard a great voice out of heaven saying, Behold, the <u>tabernacle of God</u> is with men, and he will dwell with them, and they shall be his people, and God himself shall be with them, and be their God."

(Revelations 21:3).

The words **"tabernacle of God"** means the same as "the abode of God," which Word is the same as the Greek word Heaven. The Kingdom of Heaven is the abode of God; it is the place where the Lord dwells, in the Kingdom of Heaven the will of God prevails. It is the place where happiness, healing and Joy prevail. This is the place where Dunamis the supernatural power of God reigns.

"And God shall wipe away all tears from their eyes; and there shall be no more death, neither sorrow, nor crying, neither shall there be any more pain..."

(Revelations 21:4).

The will of God in the Kingdom of Heaven is no more death, no more sorrow, no more crying. In the Kingdom of Heaven the Lord wipes out all the tears. When the Kingdom of Heaven settles in your life the miraculous becomes a reality in your life. The Kingdom of Heaven comes from the Holy Spirit, the Holy Spirit brings the will of God on earth, thereby wiping away all pain, sickness and sorrow. The Kingdom of Heaven brings the supernatural into our lives; it starts angelic activities as well as giving us a heavenly language to use when dealing with the heavenlies. The scripture declares that we are sitted in Christ in the Heavenly places.

> *"And hath raised us up together, and made us sit together in heavenly places in Christ Jesus."*
>
> *(Ephesians 2:6).*

The Kingdom of Heaven brings spiritual blessings to us, in this Kingdom there is heavenly provision for all things. Ephesians 1:3 shows us that this Kingdom come with supernatural blessings. Heaven has no lack, there is neither worry nor poverty, when the Kingdom of Heaven appears in your life; lack, worry and poverty disappears.

> *"Blessed be the God and father of our Lord Jesus Christ, who hath blessed us with all spiritual blessings in the heavenly places in Christ."*
>
> *(Ephesians 1:3).*

We access the power and the blessing from the Kingdom of Heaven IN CHRIST. Whenever the scripture says in Christ just know that it's from the Kingdom of Heaven. God reconciles us to Himself IN CHRIST. God the father reaches out to us in

Christ Jesus, we reach to God the father in the name of Jesus Christ.

We can only receive all the provisions and the power from the Kingdom of Heaven if we BELIEVE!!!!!

Believing commits God's integrity; it is only when you believe that you put God at a place of no choice but to fulfill His word. The scripture in the gospel of Mathew brings this revelation clearly though in a negative sense. But clearly shows that if you can see with your eyes, and hear with your ears the reality of the Word of God which is to perceive. And if you understand with your heart, then all things are possible with you. This is the scriptural meaning of believing, to perceive and understand the reality of the Word of God.

> "And in them is fulfilled the prophecy of Esaias, which saith, By hearing ye shall hear, and shall not perceive: For this people's hearts is waxed gross, and their ears are dull of hearing, and their eyes they have closed; lest at any time they should see with their eyes, and hear with their ears, and should understand with their hearts, and should be converted, and I SHOULD HEAL them."
>
> *(Mathew 13:14-15).*

The above scripture shows us that believing changes us, meaning when you believe you get converted into righteousness *(Romans 10:10)*. Righteousness puts you in line to receive from heaven; you become a candidate to receive from heaven. The highlighted words *"I should heal them,"* denotes that God will have no choice but to give you the provisions of heaven like healing in this case; because by believing and acting on what you believe you commit God's integrity.

4

Kings and Priests

"And hast made us unto our God Kings and Priests: and we shall reign on earth."

(Revelations 5:10).

From the times of old, the Lord God had always used kings and priests to rule this earth. He started with King Saul there always Priests in the house of Israel from the time of Aaron the high Priest. The priests in the house of Israel were ambassadors representing the kingdom of heaven. If you take an audit of the temple of old, you will find that it is a replica of heaven and the priests always had a place in the temple. The temple represented heaven and the priests represented God. The King on the other hand was placed by God to administer Justice, Peace and to thwart other forms of worship that may have come from other kingdoms. The King therefore represented the legal side of the just God; he represented God's mercy, His mighty, his fatherly love and His Lordship over the affairs of the earth. The Priest represented the spiritual side of God. The priests represented his loving-kindness; His grace forgiveness of sin, providing healing and all the amenities from heaven. Both Kings and Priests are called by God and anointed by the Holy Spirit to carry out their respective duties. The same happened with us when we were called, saved and anointed by the Holy Spirit.

For this reason the Lord of heaven and earth has made us Kings and Priests unto Himself so that we might reign on earth. The Lord has called us to be ambassadors on earth; He has called us to represent his rule (the Kingdom of God and the Kingdom of Heaven) on earth. He has therefore called us to be Kings to represent the Kingdom of God and Priests to represent the Kingdom of Heaven. He has given us EXOUSIA (divine authority) to reign as Kings and DUNAMIS (miraculous power) to reign as Priests. We are made Kings by the word at work in us and we are made Priests by the anointing of the Holy Spirit at work in us.

Kings

"Where the word of a King is there is POWER:..."
(Ecclesiastes 8:4).

Kings rule with Words, the power of Kings is invested in their Word. The power of your Word represents your strength as a King. Kings operate in and with the Kingdom of God; this implies the rulership of God and the authority of God found in his Word. We operate in and with the

AUTHORITY (exousia) of King Jesus Christ of Nazareth in whom all power (exousia) was given.

> *"And Jesus came and spake unto them, saying, ALL POWER (exousia) is given unto me in heaven and in earth."*

(Mathew 28:18).

This is the same power that was delegated to us, to operate in us Kings. This is the same power that was given to us to overcome all the forces of darkness. The Lord Jesus in the scriptural passage of *Luke 10:19* gave a powerful handover of delegated authority, as shown below:

> *"Behold, I give unto you POWER (exousia) to tread on serpents and scorpions, and over all the POWER (dunamis) of the enemy:......"*

The passage above shows that we have authority or power over the dunamis of the enemy, meaning we have power over the miraculous powers of the evil one. This implies that we have power over the demonic powers, witchcraft, sorcery, Satanism, occultism and or any form of magic. In Jesus we have the Exousia to thwart all the powers, rulers and principalities in high places of the Kingdom of Darkness and the Kingdoms of this world. The scripture in *(2 Corinthians 10:4)* declares that *"the weapons of our warfare are not carnal (man made) but mighty (powerful) through God (the kingdom of God,*

the word of God) to the pulling down of strongholds."
"Mighty through God means "mighty through the Exousia" the authority in the word of God. The strongholds in high places are hubs for spiritual wickedness. For this reason we cannot use the power to witness the (Dunamis) to thwart the powers of darkness, we need the authority of the Kingdom of light; the Kingdom of God to thwart the powers of the Kingdom of darkness.
This authority is the Exousia, the authority found in the word of God.

Ephesians 6:17 clarifies that the weapon of our warfare is the sword of the Spirit, which is the Word of God (the exousia in the Kingdom of God).

The key to all the EXOUSIA (authority) in the Kingdom of God is the NAME JESUS. In this name, we can access all authority and power over all the powers in heaven, in earth and under the earth. This Name unleashes all of the EXOUSIA available!

"That at the name of JESUS every knee SHOULD bow, of things in heaven, and things in earth, and things under the earth."
(Philippians 2:10).

Many have misinterpreted this scripture, because of bible interpreters have used the word shall instead of should, basing on this; many have interpreted it to mean that every knee shall bow at the second coming of our Lord Jesus. This is not so, the correct word is **SHOULD bow**, which means it is **LAW**. At the name Jesus, every knee bows of things in heaven, things in earth and things in hell TODAY!

Examples of Kings:

The Lord by His sovereignty causes some to function more as kings and yet others function more as priests. One Powerful man of God who I believe has been crafted by the Lord to function as a King is Pastor Chris Oyakhilome. I love this man he is my spiritual father and he is a King in his function. Many times when you see him during his healing ministry you would see that he uses the power of his (Rhema) word to heal the sick. During his healing services called the Healing School, you will see how much power and authority he exercises on the infirmities and the evil spirits tormenting people. Pastor Chris uses EXOUSIA in the Kingdom of God to thwart all manner of diseases and infirmities. He is a King who has found his place in the Kingdom of God.

The other aspect of his Kingship is the Spirit of excellence; I attended one of his conferences dubbed the Night of Bliss, in Johannesburg South Africa in March 2008. I was privileged to be appointed as one of the security team members; this gave me a chance to appreciate the excellence with which they carry out their ministry. It is so incredible. This man is a King, who knows his authority, not just against the Kingdom of Darkness but also against the Kingdom of the world.

Priests

"For the Priest's lips keep knowledge, and they should seek the law at his mouth: for he is a messenger of the LORD of hosts."
(Malachi 2:7).

The lips of Priests carry revelation, this is the power of priests; the knowledge of the will of the Kingdom of Heaven. The scripture above declares that priests are messengers of the Lord. A messenger is as good as an ambassador. An ambassador to the world is not from the world; he is just here to represent the affairs of heaven on earth. Priests operate in and from the Kingdom of Heaven; they operate with DUNAMIS, which comes from the Holy Spirit.

"But ye shall receive power (dunamis), after that the Holy Ghost is come upon you: and ye shall be witnesses unto me........."
(Acts 1:8).

The Holy Spirit gives us power to perform our priestly duties. The Holy Spirit gives us strength to spread the will of God on earth as well as power to manifest the Kingdom of Heaven in people's lives. By manifesting the Kingdom of Heaven, I mean bringing freedom into people's lives, freedom from sickness, feebleness, disease and pain. The Holy Spirit brings the Kingdom of Heaven on earth, He brings healing and deliverance.

"Now the Lord is that Spirit: and where the Spirit of the Lord is, there is Liberty."
(2 Corinthians 3:17).

The word Liberty also means freedom, so where the Spirit of the Lord is there is freedom from the Bondage of sickness, feebleness and disease. The Power at work in the Spirit of the Lord is the Dunamis, the miraculous power, and the power that bestows heaven on earth. It bestows the will of God in the Kingdom of Heaven on earth. ***Revelations 21:4*** declares that there is no pain, sickness and death in heaven, the same happens when the Kingdom of Heaven descends in a place by the Holy Spirit.

When the Kingdom of Heaven by the Holy Spirit lives in you, he gives you the powers to bring heaven into the place were you are. The same is said about the Lord Jesus when He started His public ministry as recorded in the Gospel of ***Luke 4:18-19.*** The Lord declared that the anointing (power) of the Holy Spirit is upon me, and has given me power to be a priest and bring heaven into peoples lives. This is the summary of what was recorded in the Gospel of Luke.

> *"The Spirit of the Lord is upon me, because he hath anointed me to preach the gospel to the poor; he hath sent me to heal the brokenhearted, to preach deliverance to the captives, and recovering of sight to the blind, to set at liberty them that are bruised, To preach the acceptable year of the Lord."*

I believe every Priest has been given power by the Holy Spirit to do the above-mentioned things, to bring the Kingdom of Heaven in people's lives.
It is the job description of every priest to function like this. Priests have the responsibility of bringing heaven in people's lives; they are ambassadors and envoys of peace from heaven. Priests have also been given power to intercede for the saints; to stand in the gap for the whole body of Christ, so that the Kingdom of Heaven may reign in the lives of the saints as shown below:

> *"Praying always with all prayer and supplication in the Spirit, and watching thereunto with all perseverance and supplication for all saints."*
>
> *(Ephesians 6:18).*

This is our priestly duty to be ambassadors of the Kingdom of Heaven and to pray for the saints in the Spirit so that the Kingdom of Heaven may reign in the church.

Examples of Priests:

Pastor Benny Hinn is one of the men of God I believe to be an example of a priest. Pastor Benny operates so much in the Kingdom of Heaven, when you pay closer attention to his message you will realize that he is a heavenly being so in love with the Holy Spirit. His message so much brings the mysteries of Heaven to us; than our position in Christ. He is so powerful a man of God. I believed in the power of the Holy Spirit from his ministry, he's such an awesome man of God full of humility and power.

Pastor Benny during his healing meetings demonstrates the power (Dunamis) of the Kingdom of Heaven in the Holy Spirit. He would just be worshiping and the Kingdom of Heaven descends in the place where he is having the meeting, then all that are sick and believe are healed. Not all are healed, even when the Kingdom of Heaven manifests because it is impossible to receive anything from Heaven if you do not believe!

You are a King and a Priest

"And hath made us Kings and Priests unto God and his father; to him be glory and dominion for ever and ever Amen."

(Revelations 1:6).

The Lord Jesus has made us Kings and Priests so that we may bring Glory to his father. He (the Lord Jesus) has made us Kings and Priests to exercise dominion on earth on behalf the father. The Lord called us all, to be kings and priests unto himself, so that we may reign on earth. You are designed to function as a king and a priest from the moment you are born again.

Through the Word of God working in you, you receive power (EXOUSIA) to be a king and with the Holy Spirit working in you; you receive power (DUNAMIS) to be a priest. The two men of God; pastor Chris Oyakhilome and pastor Benny Hinn are both Kings and Priests, I just got a segment of their respective ministries to explain the function ability of the Kingdom of Heaven and Kingdom of God; Priestly ministry and Kingly ministry. Minister like a priest; pray like a priest but talk like a King; think like a King and act like a King.

The Word at work in you makes you a King and the anointing of the Holy Spirit in you makes you a Priest. Every one born of God is a King and a Priest; this is because you are born of the Word and the Spirit of God. ***"Being born again, not of corruptible seed, but of incorruptible; by the <u>word of God</u>, which liveth and abideth forever." (1 Peter 1:23).***

"The wind bloweth where it listeth, and thou hearest the sound thereof, but canst not tell whence it cometh, and whither it goeth: so is everyone that is <u>born of the spirit.</u>"

(John 3:8).

5

How to function in the two-fold Authority

By now I believe that you know that you were called to function both as a King and a Priest. This level of operation is also referred to as the most holy faith. In the book of *Jude 20*, the most holy faith is attained through praying in the Holy Spirit (tongues). Faith comes from the word of God, so the working of the word of God and the Holy Spirit in you produces the most holy faith for you.

The working of the word of God in you produces a King in you; well the working of the Holy Spirit in you produces a priest in you. This means that for you to appropriate to yourself the two-fold power to work as a King and a Priest you have to have the word of God and the Holy Spirit in you.

The word of God and the Holy Spirit comes to you as a seed. This seed has to die and then germinate in you. Then this seed must grow in you until it becomes a tree. This tree must grow to maturity, so that it can produce fruits. In the fruits is where you find seeds. As a King and a Priest your authority and power is in your fruit. A fully-grown fruit produces seeds in it and it is in the fruit that you give or plant seeds. In that fruit as you exercise your authority and power in Christ you also plant seeds of the word of God and the Holy Spirit in others. In other words you cannot give what you don't have. You first need to have the fruit of the Kingdom of God and the Kingdom of Heaven in order for you to give the Kingdom authority and power. For the authority and power is found in the fruit, so work out your salvation in you to produce the fruit of Priestly and Kingly power and authority respectively.

You need to work it out your salvation in Christ for you to operate effectively as a King and a Priest.

There are two ways in which this is attained. The first one is studying and meditating on the word of God; and the second one is having the Holy Spirit and praying in tongues. This order must always be followed, as there is no prayer without the word of God.

"Study to shew thyself approved unto God, a workman that needeth not to be ashamed, rightly dividing the word of truth."

(2 Timothy 2:15).

Many in the body of Christ, pray a lot but don't study and meditate on the word of God. Many still don't understand the mystery of praying in tongues and therefore don't pray in tongues. For this reason many don't function in the authority of Kings and the power of Priests. This is because they miss the importance of the Word of God and the Holy Spirit.

Meditation

"This book of the law shall not depart from thy mouth; but thou shall MEDITATE therein day and night, that thou mayest observe to do according to all that is written therein: for then shalt make thy way prosperous, and then thou shalt have good success."

(Joshua 1:8).

The word used for meditate is a Hebrew word **"HAGAH"**. This Word Hagah implies to ponder study, mutter, imagine, speak, talk and utter, following the implication of this Word rather than the meaning in English language gives us a more detailed account of what meditation really means in action. I re- arranged the words a bit to start with the word **study, ponder, imagine, mutter, utter, speak and talk** this explanation of meditation is given in order to give an understanding of meditation as an art.

Study

First: Study the Word, don't be in the habit of just reading the Word of God as a by the way activity. Drop the mindset of just going through what pastor taught and thinking that studying is only for pastors, you have to study if you are to function as a King. Know this; we are all called to be Kings and Priest unto the Lord and not just pastors. *"It is the glory of God to conceal a thing: but the honour of Kings is to search out a matter." (Proverbs 25:2).* So searching out a matter in the scriptures is honourable to you as a king, unto him who has called us unto Himself to the praise of His Glory.

Ponder

Second: Ponder on the Word; to ponder is to dwell on the word. This implies dissecting the word trying to understand the revelation behind the word, you may need to go through the same passage many times and also study different versions of the scriptures in order to get the mind of God and not just the written word. Know that you don't have to know everything in the scriptures, but make sure that the little you know is working in you. You can study a chapter or just a few verse but just make sure you get your now word. This might mean going to the original languages used like Hebrew and Greek to get the exact wording used. You may also need to read the commentaries in order to get the revelation.

One night I dreamed someone was explaining to me *Colossians 3:1-4*; this scripture stayed with me for a long time, I was just pondering on it day after day, it took me about a week or two of just studying and pondering the same passage of scripture, until one day it all opened up. It made a great deal of sense and it is the word that became the corner stone of my life and ministry. Now I know my place in the Kingdom because of pondering on the word. Glory to God!!! Ponder on the word of God and get your place known.

Imagine

Third: Imagine the Word; to imagine is to make a mental picture of the word. Christ Jesus is the manifested word of God into flesh *(John 1:14).* So you should know what the Word at work looks like, it looks like the person and life of Jesus. When for instance you are studying on the passage where the Lord Jesus healed someone of any disease or evil spirits, try to make a picture in your mind of how he did it. The more you spend time thinking and imagining something the more you fall in love with the same thing, so if you spend more time thinking and imagining on how the word worked in the time of Jesus' earthly ministry you will fall in love with the idea of the word working the same way in your life and that can be a good start for great things.

Mutter

Fourth: Mutter the Word; to mutter is to speak under your breath. After you have a mental picture of the word you get some understanding or enlightenment and therefore you start speaking the word under your breath. You continue muttering the word, until the authority of the word starts to take over you. The more you mutter the more you fill your heart warming up with the power of the word. This will give you unusual energy, and you will unconsciously start rising up you voice and before you know it, you will be filled with joy and peace.

Utter

Fifth: Utter the word; to utter is to speak with an audible voice. As your voice starts rising from muttering the word you automatically get into uttering the word with a loud voice. This process will convince your heart and change the course of your life. The more you utter the word into your ears the more it changes you. It is a seed that gets straight into a fertile ground. This process deals with speaking the exact word in the scripture into your ears and heart; it deals with the logos, the written word of God. When the word sinks into your heart it will move you to start speaking the word to your self, and for your exact situation.

Speak

Sixth: Speak the Word; to speak is to talk with insight. After the word fills your heart, your heart will start channeling the course of your life with the word. ***"A man's heart deviseth his way..." (Proverbs 16:9).*** It will course you to speak to yourself concerning the word. ***"…..for out of the abundance of the heart the mouth speaketh." (Mathew 12:34).*** Rhema will start coming out of your mouth. Rhema is the living Word coming from a heart that is filled with the word of God. This is the now Word you speak concerning your situation, it is the Word of authority. The Lord Jesus used the Rhema Word against the devil when he saw that the devil was attacking him with logos (the written Word). He said **"it is SAID."** in *(Luke 4:12)* the previous times he answered it is written.

Talk

Seventh: Talk the word; to talk is to discuss with another, always have friends you can share your revelations with. This act of sharing gives you even more clarity, it is when am sharing that I get even more revelations. Today I am able to write this book because I have people to share my revelations with. There is power in sharing, the more you give the more you receive is true. I have experienced this more in the area of revelations than in the area of money, but I believe it is a principle that works everywhere in the Kingdom of God.

Praying in other Tongues

"He that speaks in an unknown tongue edifies himself."

(1 Corinthians 14:4).

Praying in tongues creates for you the opportunity to grow spiritually. The word "edifies" means to build or construct a superstructure. This then means that as you pray in other tongues you are building a superstructure in the Spirit. This will help you work in the power (dunamis) of the Holy Spirit as this stirs up the anointing in you; it makes you function in the higher realms of the Spirit. Tongues like meditation are a way of growing the seed of the Holy Spirit in us, to produce the anointing or the power to work as a priest.

"That he would grant you, according to the riches of his glory, to be strengthened with might (Dunamis) by his Spirit in the inner man."

(Ephesians 3:16).

The strengthening of the inner man by his Spirit is done through praying in tongues. The Word "might" as used in the scripture above is a Greek word Dunamis. This then means that the inner man is strengthened with Dunamis, the miraculous power through speaking in tongues. This is what the scripture means in *(1 Corinthians 14:4).*

The Living Bible tells us that the one who speaks in tongues **"helps himself grow spiritually,"** this means that for you to experience serious spiritual growth; you must pray in tongues consistently. I have received a lot of revelations during praying in tongues; this to me has been my source of insight.

Whenever I don't have understanding concerning a matter in life or about a passage of scripture I quickly go to praying in tongues for solutions.

Power of Tongues for Edification

(extracted from "Tongues of Angels Unveiled").

"He that speaketh in an unknown tongue edifieth himself..."

(1 Corinthians 14:4).

Edification comes from a Greek word **"Oikodomeo"** that means among others *building a concrete structure, and to embolden.* This then means through speaking in tongues we can construct from our spirit, soul and body a supernatural structure. We open our bodies to supernatural health, our lives to more of the realities of the spiritual as we speak more in tongues.

Speaking in tongues has the power to take us to a large place in the spiritual realm. In this place, our eyes of understanding open more to the realities of the heavelies where we are sitted in Christ. We become aware of our inheritance and take our proper place of authority in Christ, when we come to a large place. The large place is a place of honour; it is a place of blessings. The story of the man called Jabez gives us an example of a man who understood the benefits of operating from the large place, the place of authority and influence. Here is the summary of Jabez's story as recorded in 1st chronicles 4:9-10.

> And Jabez was more honourable than his brethren: and his mother called his name Jabez, saying, Because I bare him with sorrow. And Jabez called on the God of Israel, saying, Oh that thou wouldest bless me indeed, and enlarge my coast, and that thine hand might be with me, and that thou wouldest keep me from evil, that it may not grieve me! And God granted him that which he requested.

From the story of Jabez we can tell that in the large place there is a heavy anointing. We can also tell that there is grace to protect us from evil and sin. The edification that we get in tongues brings us to the large place. Influence, a heavy anointing settles on our lives and grace to overcome sin and evil. Like Jabez, the Lord can grant us this large territory as we pray in tongues.

> "He brought me forth also into a large place; he delivered me, because he delighted in me. The LORD rewarded me according to my righteousness; according to the cleanness of my hands hath he recompensed me.

For I have kept the ways of the LORD, and have not wickedly departed from my God. For all his judgments were before me, and I did not put away his statutes from me. I was also upright before him, and I kept myself from mine iniquity. Therefore hath the LORD recompensed me according to my righteousness, according to the cleanness of my hands in his eyesight. With the merciful thou wilt shew thyself merciful; with an upright man thou wilt shew thyself upright; With the pure thou wilt shew thyself pure; and with the froward thou wilt shew thyself froward. For thou wilt save the afflicted people; but wilt bring down high looks. For thou wilt light my candle: the LORD my God will <u>enlighten my darkness</u>. For by thee I have <u>run through a troop</u>; and by my God have I <u>leaped over a wall</u>. As for God, his way is perfect: the word of the LORD is tried: he is a buckler to all those that trust in him. For who is God save the LORD? or who is a rock save our God? It is God that <u>girdeth me with strength, and maketh my way perfect.</u> He maketh my feet like <u>hinds' feet</u>, and setteth me upon my high places. He teacheth my <u>hands to war</u>, so that a bow <u>of steel is broken by mine arms</u>.

Thou hast also given me the <u>shield of thy salvation</u>: and thy right hand hath holden me up, and thy <u>gentleness hath made me great</u>. {thy gentleness...: or, with thy meekness thou <u>hast multiplied me</u>} Thou hast <u>enlarged my steps under me that my feet did not slip</u>. I have pursued mine enemies, and <u>overtaken them</u>: neither did I turn again till they were consumed. I have wounded them that they were not able to rise: they are fallen under my feet. For thou hast <u>girded me with strength unto the battle</u>: thou hast subdued under me those that rose up against

The above scripture gives us a clear picture of what it means to be in a large place. Speaking in tongues takes us to this large place, as we receive edification. The highlights of the above scripture give us about 14 places where the Lord builds us in this process of edification.

Let's go through the 14 highlighted places of the above scripture and study in detail what the Lord wants to accomplish in you through the process of speaking in tongues. In the above scripture, we see that as speak more in tongues the Lord begins to **enlighten areas of darkness** in our lives. The Amplified Bible puts it more clearly like this; **"For you cause my lamp to be lighted and to shine; the Lord my God illuminates my darkness."** The lamp is the

Word of God in your life *(Psalms 119:105)*. As you speak more in tongues, the Word of God in you starts to shine and discern areas of darkness in your life. The Word will lighten dark areas and bring life in every area of your life.

Then He will give you the ability through tongues to *"run through a troop"* which is the wall that was shutting you in. You receive by the Spirit through tongues ability to run through situations that in the past have held you prisoner. The Lord by the Spirit through speaking in tongues also gives the ability to *"leap over a wall."* This is the ability to jump over the walls of limitations. He shall also *"buckle you with strength"* in your character by the Word and *"make your ways perfect"* as you speak more in tongues. The Lord will give you *"hind's feet"* meaning He will give you the ability to stand firm and make progress in dangerous heights of testing and trouble.

The Lord will through the process of edification *"teach your hands to war,"* so that you can be able to *"break the bow of steel"* by your hands. This strength is for spiritual warfare to quench the arrows and attacks of the devil that you receive as you speak more in tongues. The right hand of the Lord *becomes the shield of your salvation* and the gentleness of the Lord *becomes your greatness*. As you speak more in tongues, the Lord *"enlarges our steps and makes them firm."* This enlarging of your steps is spiritual expedience. You begin to do things at a supernatural speed. Just like Prophet Elijah, out-ran horses in his days you begin to out-run your odds. Things you do gain divine speed and expedience. This then gives you the ability to overtake.

The large place is a place of spiritual strength and of supernatural occurrences. It is a place of greatness, enlarged steps, supernatural stability and speed.

Speak more in tongues and enter into in your large place! Live the supernatural life naturally! Glory to the highest!

The Seed of Power

"Behold, I give unto you power to tread on serpents and scorpions, and over all the power of the enemy: and nothing shall by any means hurt you."

(Luke 10:19).

The scripture above declares that the Lord Jesus has given us power (exousia) to overcome the works of the enemy. This power given to believers, the moment we are born again. Hence, the reason why the Lord Jesus in **Mark 16:17** declared that believers shall cast out devils, shall lay hands on the sick and the sick shall be healed.

"He that believeth and is baptized shall be saved; but he that believeth not shall be damned. And these signs shall follow them that believe; In my name shall they cast out devils; they shall speak with new tongues; They shall take up serpents; and if they drink any deadly thing, it shall not hurt them; they shall lay hands on the sick, and they shall recover."

(Mark 16:16-18).

This authority given to every believer as recorded in the above scripture comes in seed form. In this form, the authority is too weak to work for you and have the maximum results. For this seed to grow and manifest in you, you need to do the godly exercise of praying in the Spirit and meditating on the Word of God. The word power in the above scripture comes from a root word **"EXOUSIA."** Exousia is a Greek word that means among other words Competency and Mastery.

This means the Lord has given us competency and mastery in our spirit against the forces of darkness. However, we have to grow the seed of competency and mastery through the process of speaking in tongues and meditation on the Word of God in order to be competent and masters over the works of the enemy. We must grow the seed of power in us to overcome the miraculous and demonic powers of the enemy.

The other word used for power is the Greek word **"DUNAMIS,"** this word means miraculous power. This is the power to do God's work. This power also comes in seed form. This is the mystery behind the miraculous, the seed aspect of the power given by the Holy Spirit.

> "But ye shall receive POWER (DUNAMIS), after that the Holy Ghost is come upon you:........."
>
> *(Acts 1:8).*

> "And behold, I send the promise of my father upon you: but tarry ye in the city of Jerusalem, until ye be endued with POWER (DUNAMIS) from on high."
>
> *(Luke 24:49).*

Many believers in the body of Christ have received the Holy Spirit in their lives but only few function in the miraculous power. This is because not many have the understanding that speaking in tongues or praying in the Spirit grows the seed of the miraculous and gives the ability to do the wonderful works of God. The Dunamis gives you the ability to be a witness for Christ. It gives the ability to perform miracles, signs and wonders. This ability however comes in seed form and can only be increased through the processes of meditation on the Word and speaking in tongues.

Speaking in tongues is a mystery that unlocks the miraculous as well as gives you mastery over the forces of darkness and the wisdom of this world.

Roots Us in Love

The scriptures declare that the Holy Spirit poured the love of God in our hearts. This love in our hearts came in seed-form, can only grow, and be fully comprehended if we speak more in tongues.

".........because the love of God is shed abroad in our hearts by the Holy Ghost which is given to us."

(Romans 5:5).

The love shed in our hearts is a seed of love. This seed needs to be natured in order to grow in our lives. The full manifestation of this love shed in our hearts is the manifestation of Christ in our lives. This is because Christ is the manifested love of God.

"But after that the kindness and the Love of God our saviour toward man appeared."

(Titus 3:4).

Tongues are a mysterious tool the Holy Spirit uses to strengthen our inner man with mighty and causing the seed of love to be natured in our hearts. Every gift given by the Holy Spirit can only natured and matured by the Holy Spirit. And this done through the tool of speaking in tongues.

> *"For this cause I bow my knees unto the father of our Lord Jesus Christ, Of whom the whole family in heaven and earth is named, That he would grant you according to the riches of his glory, to be strengthened with MIGHT (Dunamis) by his Spirit in the inner man, That Christ may dwell in your hearts by faith; that ye , being rooted and grounded in love may be able to comprehend with all saints what is the breadth, and the length, and depth, and height, And to KNOW (gnosko) the love of Christ, which passeth KNOWLEDGE (gnosis), that ye might be filled all the fullness of God."*
>
> *(Ephesians 3:14-19).*

Through speaking more in tongues the Holy Spirit strengthens our inner man with mighty translated as Dunamis in Greek. This means that our inner man get strengthened with the miraculous power that causes us to understand and know the full measure of the love of Christ.

The word **"know"** in the above passage of scripture comes from a Greek word **"GINOSKO"** which means having absolute knowledge, having a good perception, a good understanding in the Spirit of the love of Christ. On the contrary, the word **"knowledge"** in the scripture above comes from a root word **"GNOSIS"** which means scientific knowledge. This is the knowledge based on the scientific evidence of the understanding of the love of Christ. This knowledge is a lower kind of knowledge based on mental or physical understanding of the love of Christ. God is Spirit and a natural mind cannot comprehend His love. A natural man cannot have deep understanding of the love of God. Unless man has absolute knowledge only given by the Holy Spirit, he cannot understand the love of God.

The strengthening of the inner man by the Holy Spirit through the exercise of speaking in tongues produces the ability to grow the love of Christ in you. As you speak more in tongues, you are rooted and grounded in love. You understand the breadth, the length, the depth and the height of the love of God. Then you get to know the fullness of God in your spirit. Strengthen your inner man through constantly praying in tongues!

Builds Your Faith into the Most Holy Faith

"But ye, beloved, building up yourselves on your most holy faith, Praying in the Holy Ghost."

(Jude 20).

The words building up come from a Greek word **"epoikodomeo,"** which means to build upon. This then means that as you pray in tongues you begin to build upon your faith, the most holy faith. This is the highest level of faith one can operate in. Build your faith upon the rock, which is the purity of the holiness of the Word of God.

A Royal Priesthood

The combination of meditating on the Word of God and Speaking in Tongues makes you a royal priest. You become a Kingly Priest because you have authority and wisdom over the system of the world and power over the Kingdom of darkness. You also have influence in the heavens. The only people who can please God the father are those who walk in the Spirit as Priests and those who live by faith as Kings.

We are a royal priesthood, a kingly priest. A priest and a king set apart by God the father himself for us to reign in this life on his behalf. He has given us Priestly and Kingly positions to represent his interests on earth.

Remember that royalty is always given more attention both in heaven and on earth. For this reason as royalty our prayers, requests, petitions are given more attention in heaven, they are given more priority. That is the reason why we can petition God the father concerning things in his Word.

Wisdom, treasure and wealth are given to Kings. This is given for them to rule with justice. As a king God has laid up treasures for you. That's why the scripture advises us to seek the Kingdom of God and his righteousness, and then everything will be added to us.

Every man is a priest over his house, and therefore God gave you heavenly power to bless you wife and children. You are a King and a Priest: you are the strong man in your household; no one can enter your house unless you allow him and/ or you are ignorant of your Kingly and Priestly authority. But you also have another priest who is your high Priest the Lord Jesus Christ; He is also our King and therefore is called the King of Kings.

Application of the two-fold Power

The application of the two-fold power has created a lot of confusion in the church today. Many do not have the revelation of the difference in the two-fold power. Many still use DUNAMIS and EXOUSIA interchangeably. You have to realize that this two-fold power has rules. There are rules for operating with dunamis as well as operating with exousia. Dunamis is the power given for priestly duties and Exousia is the power given for Kingly duties. If you use them interchangeably you will not appreciate them so much.

Dunamis is the miraculous power that comes from the Holy Spirit. This power is to enable us witness to the world the gospel of our Lord Jesus Christ. This power comes in form of an anointing to preach, to teach, to prophesy and to heal among others. All the gifts and abilities given by the Holy Spirit are given effect by Dunamis, the power of the Holy Spirit. Dunamis therefore is the power to enforce our ministry giftings. As we witness about the resurrection of our lord Jesus Christ.

"And with great power (Dunamis) gave the apostles witness of the resurrection of the Lord Jesus: and great grace was upon them all."

(Acts 4:33).

The apostles witnessed with the power of the Holy Ghost through miracles, signs and wonders. Through preaching the Gospel with gusto and teaching the oracles of God with clarity. Preaching and teaching with signs and wonders accompanying the preaching of the Gospel. The power of the Holy Spirit, the Dunamis or the anointing as popularly known is for the work of spreading the Gospel. This power is for witnessing to the resurrected Christ through teaching the Word and healing the sick, demonstrating the Word with miracles, sign s and wonders.

This power is not for casting out devils. It is for bringing heaven on earth. It is for bringing the powers of the world to come into the present day *(Hebrews 6:5).*

Exousia on the other hand is the power over the kingdoms, wisdoms and Dunamis of the devil and the world. Exousia is the power that is given to us to tread over serpents and scorpions which are forms of demon spirits. The power to overcome and or drive out demon spirits is the exousia, the power of the Word of God. When faced with a clash of authority, exousia is the power to overcome all other authorities that do not come from Jesus. We like Jesus also have authority over nature with the power of exousia *(Mark 4:39).* We have authority to forgive sin by the same exousia *(John 20:23).*

> *But that ye may know that the Son of man hath power on earth to forgive sins, (he saith to the sick of the palsy,)*
>
> (Mark 2:10).

The scripture above says *"but that you know that the son of man has power (exousia) on earth to forgive sins."* This power or authority to forgive sin was given to the sons of men. Jesus operated here on earth as a man. Any son of man with this exousia has power to forgive sins and that sin shall be forgiven. This son of man can be you and me. Remember that Jeremiah was referred to as the son of man and so is Ezekiel. *"And he said unto me, SON OF MAN, stand upon thy feet, and I will speak unto thee." (Ezekiel 2:1).*

If the Lord called Ezekiel son of man who was a man like us, then He also saw Jesus a man like us when referred to Him as a son of man. This therefore means that whatever authority Jesus had as a son of man we have as sons of men. Whatever Jesus could do as a son of man on earth we can also do because we have the same Holy Ghost Jesus had and the same authority He had as a son of man. That's why the Lord Jesus in *John 20 :23* He said *"Whoever's sins you forgive, they are forgiven them. Whoever's sins you retain, they have been retained."*

Recently I heard a very sad story of the misuse or the misunderstanding of the two fold power. From the story as narrated by my wife and sister in law. There was a teenage girl who was possessed with demon spirits. This girl was taken to her pastor's house for prayer. I don't know how exactly things went but when they were praying for the girl they started hitting her. They subsequently broke her ribs and she eventually died of the wounds. The pastor and his helper are now arrested for murder. This is a common mistake in the body of Christ. Demons do not respond to physical strength, they respond to the authority in your words. I have seen many times people pining down a person possessed by demon spirits and even hitting the person in the name of beating the demon. The demon only takes over the will and soul of the person. If therefore you hit the body pain will be felt after the whole ordeal. This so called no nonsense approach to demons or persons possessed with demons has led to many inflicting bodily harm to the person they were praying for.

Exousia which is the authority over demon spirits is in the power of your words and not in your physical strength. We do not wrestle flesh and blood *(Ephesians 6:12).* When the demon spirit charges against you with strength using the body of the person possessed you cannot fight back in the physical. It is the same demon spirit that has control over an innocent soul and causing him or her to do such things. One thing to always remember is that the spirit controlling this person doesn't care what happens to him. Every demon spirit is a selfish spirit, always controlling and moving their victims to satisfy their own evil desires.

I also have seen many men of God calling "fire fire!" when it comes to the issue of demons. The fire is always related to the Holy Ghost in the scripture. The power of the Holy Ghost which is referred to as the "fire" of the Holy Ghost is the power for service. You shall receive power to be my witnesses when the Holy Ghost has come upon you *(Acts 1:8).* Therefore you cannot use the power of the Holy Spirit to cast out devils. Other men of God even go like "I'll teach you a lesson you demon!" I will burn you with the fire of the Holy Ghost. Where in the scripture did Jesus or the apostles burn the demon spirits with the fire of the Holy Spirit.

In conclusion, the Holy Spirit is for service that is to mean the power of the Holy Spirit is for the work of witnessing the love of God. And the exousia the authority of the Word of God is for overcoming the kingdoms of darkness and the world. Faith works with the authority of the Word, and we know that whatsoever is born of God overcomes the world. This is the victory that overcomes the world even our FAITH.

Application of the two-fold for Pastors

When a Pastor is on the pulpit preaching the gospel of truth, he is operating in the Kingdom of heaven in the power of the Holy Ghost the Dunamis. At the altar a Pastor is functions as a Priest. He is representing heaven in all that he says and does. At this time the man of God, functions under an anointing to witness the love of God to the congregants.

But when the pastor is out there in the world, he needs to use his Exousia, the Kingly authority to overcome the systems of the world. For instance you won't expect people to give you the same respect in the shopping mall as in your church. Even pastors need to be wise and use their Kingly authority to overcome the wicked ways of this world. You as a pastor will be faced with the same temptations as the as the other people living in this world. As a pastor you have to use wisdom to raise your children. You have authority over your household and be a strong man to protect your family from the forces of darkness. These forces can be in form systems of this world, spiritual wickedness and or political. In other words you need to overcome your odds with authority. With the same authority that you received from the lord Jesus, you have to overcome the world and its systems on a daily basis.

My Priestly commitment as a Pastor

The Lord Jesus and the Holy Ghost led me through his Word and took me to a number of scriptures in view of teaching us something about Zion and why we should open the gates of Zion to his people so that they can realize there calling and offer unto God spiritual sacrifice which is holy and acceptable. The Lord took me to a scripture in ***Hebrews 11:10; "which says by faith Abraham looked for a city which hath foundations, whose builder and maker is God."*** This city is where the father wants his people to live, anyone who is born again is born into this city, but it takes revelation knowledge of the city for one to benefit from the provisions of this city. That's why the apostle Paul wrote *"But eye has not seen, nor ear heard, neither have entered into the hearts of man, the things which God hath prepared for them that love him. But God has revealed them unto us by his spirit: for the spirit searches all things, yea, the deep things of God. For what man knoweth the things of man, save the spirit of man which is in him? Even so the things of God knoweth no man, but the spirit of God. Now we have received not the spirit of the world. But the spirit which is of God; that we may know the things which are freely given to us of God. Which things also we speak not in the words which man's wisdom teacheth, but which the Holy Ghost teacheth; comparing spiritual things with spiritual. But the natural man recieveth not the things of the spirit of God: for they are foolishness unto him: neither can he know them, because they are spiritually discerned."*

In *Hebrews 12:18;* this is confirmed when we are told that *"ye have not come unto a mount that might be touched, and that burned with fire, nor unto blackness, and darkness, and tempest, and the sound of a trumpet, and the voice of words; which voice they that heard entreated that the words should not be spoken to them any more:(for could not endure what was commanded, And if so much as a beast touch the mountain, it shall be stoned, or thrust through with a dart: and so terrible was the sight that Moses said, I exceedingly fear and quake:)*

"But ye have come unto mount Zion, and unto the city of the living God, the heavenly Jerusalem, and to an innumerable company of angels, to the general assembly and church of the firstborn which are written in heaven, and to God the judge of all, and to the spirits of just men made perfect, and to Jesus the mediator of the new covenant, and to the blood of sparkling, that speaketh better things than that of Abel." (Hebrews 12:24).

This is the place He Has brought us to, a heavenly city where we have angels, God the father, Christ Jesus, the spirits of the men who walked closely with God and the blood that pleads for our mercy at our disposal. That's why (Hebrews 4:16) says that we should come to the throne of Grace with confidence to obtain mercy, this is because we have come to a place where the blood of the messiah pleads for our mercy every time we error. Every believer was born into this place but most of them live defeated lives because they don't know about the place and others don't know how to get there.

For this reason the father gave me the mandate to show His people the city and to open the gates of Zion to His people. The Holy Ghost revealed to me that the father loves the gates of Zion so much so that He would love all his people to come through the gates to the holy mountain of God, the heavenly Jerusalem so that they can enjoy the provisions that He has for those He Has chosen into his family.

The psalmist had a revelation of the holy city when he wrote in *Psalm 87:1-7. "His foundation is in the holy mountains, The Lord loveth the gates of Zion more than all the dwellings of Jacob. Glorious things are spoken of thee, O city of God. I will make mention of Rahab and Babylon to them that know me: behold Philistia and Tyre, with Ethiopia; this man was born there.*
And of Zion it shall be said this and that one was born in her: and the Highest himself shall establish her; The Lord shall count, when he writeth up the people, that this man was born there. As well the singers as the players on instruments shall be there: all my springs are in thee."

The Lord loves the Gates of Zion more than just his people Jacob (Israel). This shows that he loves the new creation in Christ Jesus more than just Jacob. This is because he has made both to be one in Christ Jesus, both Jews and Gentiles. That's why the psalmist mentioned all these people to have being born in Zion, people like Philistia who were actually the enemy of the people of God, Tyre, Babylon and Ethiopia to symbolize that in Christ there is neither Jew nor gentile.

Upon revealing this truth to me and the sense of the great commission as recorded in (Mathew 16) I was energized by the Holy Ghost to go out and open the gates of supernatural wisdom to the world and to share the love of God in Zion; to be an ambassadors for Christ as though God were making this appeal through us to ask the world to reconcile with God. And then to take the gospel to the next level in their lives, so as to enable them to know their inheritance and live lives worth of the city of Zion.

Application of the two-fold for Professionals

By professionals I mean people in general who are pursuing a professional endeavour in life. This can mean a business man, a professional employee or employer. This also applies to all levels of employees and businessmen.

The understanding among professionals that your primary calling in life is to preach the gospel and make disciples will help you appreciate the role of the Kingly and Priestly Authority bestowed upon you. You are called to reign with the authority found in Christ Jesus in this life and from your place of employment and business. But remember one fact that we are servant Kings and therefore we use our authority to serve others and lead lives which are exemplary so as to win then to Christ.

As a professional you may operate in your Priestly office and conduct bible studies at home with your family and or at work during breaks. You are also supposed to pray for your family and all the other saints in the body of Christ in your priestly ministry. But remember that you cannot carry out your priestly duties during your working hours. You will be stealing man hours from your company, you are not paid to have bible studies but to work and meet targets. Well at work use your Kingly ministry: your servant heart, your excellence in work, the wisdom in your words, the authority and love in your conduct to minister to your colleagues.

My commitment as a Professional

I understood that God created us in Christ Jesus to do good works, to be ambassadors for him in every place we find ourselves in. The Lord ministered to me in the year 2006 that any kind of work we do is part time and the only full time job for us believers is that of being ambassadors for Him, representing Him in everything we do. For this reason when He gave this revelation I asked him for grace as written in the article I wrote in the same year to the Lord as my Prayer;

"You along are my everything and in you I put my trust. You drove my life in a way I could not think or imagine, I never at any point in my life thought that I would join Intermarket Banking Corporation (Z) Ltd (IBC) but by your grace am there. I just want to thank you Lord for you are a God at hand and not afar. I am writing this because I might forget one of these beautiful days; I pray that you guide my path every day of my life and that ***YOU BLESS IBC*** because am working there. Lord please lead me to a place of sereignity and grace in still waters every day. Order my steps as **I PREACH YOUR LOVE AT IBC.** I believe you sent me here for a purpose and that purpose is to preach your love. Make me an instrument of your love and help me work as hard as you would if you were in my place. One thing I know is that you are a God of excellence and a God whose right hand is so canning and so skillful in all you do, dear Lord slap my head with your canning right hand that I may be anointed to work under the standard of the most high. Excellence is your standard and please Lord help me achieve your standard as Joseph did in Egypt. Every day I will bless your name on high and your praises will forever be on my lips. My last words were Lord Jesus I love you so much and thank you for bringing me to IBC, where I met your wonderful creation and please help me minister to them in whichever way you show me. I LOVE YOU IBC and JESUS LOVES YOU TOO.

If anyone could ask me what ministry God had for me for professionals at IBC. It was the good news that can be divided three parts:

- Bless the place where you work from with the peace of God (Mathew 10:13).

- Minister the Love of God to your colleagues. mind you? You are the light and the salt! (Mathew 5:13; 14).

- Your work should be excellent, do all things as unto the lord.(1 Corinthians 10:31).

These revelations that God gave me and the passion of taking the Gospel to the next level with God's love made the commitments to be the force that drives my passion to produce professionals of integrity.

The Lord ministered to me about being a King and a Priest when I went to work with the Bank. I believe I was a successful King and Priest at Intermarket Banking because my life touched many people at the Bank, both clients and colleagues. I knew much earlier in life by the grace of our Lord Jesus that I have Kingly and Priestly authority in me and that I had to be intentional to operate in this authority effectively.

My Experience with Exousia

I remember sometime back in the year 2003; I had a lot of encounters with demon possessed persons. Then, I didn't have this revelation of Exousia and Dunamis. It was so hard for me to deal with the demons because I was using the wrong authority. I remember those days when I could just declare fire of the Holy Spirit on the demons. The demon would just be screaming and I could be very tired at the end of it all, my voice gone, and no strength and tired. What I didn't know is that I was using the power to do the miraculous, against the Kingdom of darkness. I was using Dunamis instead of Exousia. *"So mightily grew the word of God and prevailed."* (Acts 19:20). The Word of God when increased it overcomes with authority. To prevail is to overcome so I realized that the only way to overcome with ease is to use the Word of God.

One day during a camp meeting I was surprised at what happened, this event started my revolution in this area. It so happened that some ladies where carrying a demon possessed lady, this lady was very violent so that she gave them such a tough time trying to take her to the prayer room. When I saw what was happening, I was moved in the spirit to go and help, but when I came closer to them, I, without realizing said "BE STILL!" and the demon stopped all the violence, I was surprised at the response. This is because in the past days I had struggled with demons. The ladies were surprised too; they even put her down and ask me to pray for her. I did pray for her and the demon left in a short while. After that incidence I was prompted to find out more about these things, only to discover that I used the EXOUSIA; the authority over all the powers of darkness.(Luke 10:19).

Demons belong to the Kingdom of darkness, so if you have to thwart their powers you use your Kingly authority the exousia. To overcome all the powers of the kingdom of darkness you use the power of the Kingdom of God. The Lord Jesus used the exousia in his word to thwart the powers of darkness and to drive out the evil spirits from people. *(Mark 1:27).*

> "And they were all amazed, insomuch that they questioned among themselves, saying, What thing is this? what new doctrine is this? for with authority commandeth he even the unclean spirits, and they do obey him."

The word used for authority is the Greek Word exousia. The lord Jesus with the exousia commanded the evil spirits and they departed, even so we have been given the same authority to drive out evil spirits.

> "Behold, I give unto you POWER (exousia) to tread on serpents and scorpions, and over all the POWER (dunamis) of the enemy:......"
>
> *(Luke 10:19).*

> "And he called unto him the twelve, and began to send them forth by two and two; and gave them power(exousia) over unclean spirits."
>
> *(Mark 6:7).*

Use your Word kof power, your Rhema Word to drive out demons and not yelling "fire, fire, fire!!!!!" I have seen demons really tremble in my meetings after understanding and using this revelation. I remember one day I asked my boys to cast out a demon from a certain lady, for some time they failed to cast it out, but when I entered the prayer room the demons started begging me not to torment them and I commanded them to leave and they left at once. This has become my normal operation now; I don't struggle with demons because I know my authority, the authority to use, the exousia the authority of the Word.

Another incidence was with a woman who had 300 demon spirits in her, these were generational demons, I believe she even did some ceremonial appeasing of these spirits in times past. When I was leading her to Christ the demons manifested in her, they immediately started threatening to kill her, and then I ordered that she be taken to the prayer room. When I went to pray for her, the demons again started begging, in short I casted all the 300 demon spirits in just about a minute. This woman had gone to many deliverance ministers for deliverance, but after I prayed for her she started jumping and shouting for joy, saying she had never felt that way before, she was convinced all had gone. Glory to God!!!

There was a time when my brother bro Shadreck so gifted and anointed in many ways, was at the farm with mum, dad and our youngest sister Josephine. One day as they were walking in the farm land heading to the place where the car was packed. A stray bull (cow) charged against them.

The bull specifically targeted Shadreck and he was carrying Josephine. The parents just saw the cow in close range and screamed to Shadreck for he did not see it from afar. In response brother Shadreck charged with the knowledge of the Exousia the authority over all things just commanded the bull to stop in the name of Jesus. He just went like "stop it in the name of Jesus!" and the bull immediately stopped. It stopped as if some force just intercepted it. My father grew up as a shepherd boy, he understands how violent stray bulls can be. That time he was shocked at how the cow stopped. He said cattle only responds to the voice of the master and not a stranger. This was not Dads cow it was some stray cow from I don't know where. But at the authority given by the Word of God we have the ability to overcome any authority. The bull was intercepted by the power of the authority of the Word of God.

The authority of the Word, the exousia, causes things to change for your benefit. It has the power to make change things to your favour. I remember one day during my Lxp year. We had a fundraiser, we were asked to raise funds and find someone disadvantaged to bless. It so happened that we were all hungry as a team. So we contributed the little personal money we had. The money we put together could only get us some bread rolls, but wasn't enough to buy us cool drinks. Then I saw Nceba one of the team members speaking to one security personnel at a grocery store. I then told Valentine one of the other team members to go to that man and tell him we want cool drinks and he will give you the money. When I said this Valentine was uncomfortable with the idea, then I said okey, go and tell Nceba we need some amount for cool drinks in his presence and he will give you the money. He was at least somewhat agreeable with this. The brother did exactly what I asked him and just as I told him the man gave the exact amount I told him to the glory of God.

My Experience Functioning under Dunamis

On several occasions I have experience the power of the Holy Spirit in operation in my teaching and healing meetings. I have on many occasions experienced an external force taking over me. On many occasions I start teaching with my natural abilities, with my understanding for the first few minutes then some force would take over. When the anointing comes, my teaching changes, I would teach from the position of knowing. I would teach with much clarity and authority. I have even witnessed people shaking under the authority of my words, demon spirits manifesting and people sitting on the edge of their sits. At this moment I would learn more from what am teaching than the people listening to me. I would receive a lot of revelations and say things I would hear for the first time. Most of the things I've written in my books I have received them either when teaching or praying in tongues.

I don't usually prepare sermons and write down the points am going to teach about. This is because I always want to leave room for the teacher through His power to teach through me. In most cases I just study and meditate on the scriptures I'll be teaching on. I speak in tongues about the topic or subject I'll teaching on and meditate on the scriptures that support my subject. This is because I believe the teacher who is the Holy Spirit does not testify of Himself but of Christ who is the Word. For this reason I give the teacher who is the Holy Spirit enough raw materials which is the Word of God to use to testify about the goodness of God in Christ through my vessel. He also uses the Word in me to teach and reveal the deep and hidden things found in the Word. With the Word in me He brings and feeds faith into the hearts of the hearers. This can be faith for salvation if I am teaching on salvation, faith for healing if I am teaching on healing and so on.

I believe as a pastor one must position him/herself for the working of the power of the Holy Spirit. As for me I make sure that am in tune with the Spirit through constantly praying in tongues and that I have a good stock of the living Word of God at work in me. With this I believe I make myself available for the use by the Holy Spirit through his power to teach, to heal, to deliver and also to bring heaven in every place I find myself in.

6

The Wisdom of Performing Miracles

The mystery of performing miracles is hidden in the wisdom from on high. Miracles, signs and wonders are a natural occurrence of heaven. Here on earth they are wonders and miracles but in heaven they are the normal occurrences. *"How that he was caught up into paradise, and heard unspeakable words, which it is not lawful for a man to utter." (2Corinthians 12:4).*

The normal of heaven is unspeakable to this world. It is the naturality of the supernatural. The supernatural is natural in heaven. What we call miracles, signs and wonders are the normal occurrences in heaven. I like the way the New Living Translation of the Bible puts this; *"I was caught up to paradise and heard things so astounding that they cannot be expressed in words, things no human is allowed to tell."*

According to the scripture in NLT the things he heard were so astounding! To astound is to overwhelm with amazement. Astounding things are things capable of overwhelming with amazement; stunningly surprising. The things we call wonders and miracles are so called because they are astounding to us. They are overwhelming and stunningly surprising. These are the normal occurrences of the heavens.

The wisdom of performing miracles, signs and wonders is therefore in the effective entering in the realm of heaven. In this realm the astounding things are the normal occurrences. There are three authorities which are established in heaven. These authorities are the doorway to the life of the miraculous. These authorities bear witness of the heavenly in our lives and ministries. *"For there are three that bear record in heaven, the Father, the Word, and the Holy Ghost: and these three are one." (1John 5:7).*

The effective understanding of these three authorities is the secret to living in the miraculous.

Wisdom of Performing Miracles in the Glory Realm

The wisdom of performing miracles in the glory realm is the mystery of performing miracles with the authority of the father. The father always lives in the glory. In His glorious presence the astounding things are normal. The mystery of functioning in this authority is in the effective accessing the courts of the inner chambers of the father. No death in any form can stand in the presence of the father. Sickness, actual death, infirmities or poverty cannot stand in the presence of the glory of the father. In this realm is where a lot of supernatural angelic activities occur, supernatural provisions, divine transportation and supernatural weight loss as experienced in ministries like David Herzog's. When you effectively enter the courts of the God of heaven, the glory zone all you need is to act in faith towards what you believe Him for. Remove the eyes of the natural with its limitations and put on supernatural eyes. This will enable you to act on what believe Him for however impossible it looks in the natural realm.

The doorway into the inner courts of the God of heaven is PRAISE. The psalmist put this mystery so plainly yet it needs revelation knowledge to perceive it. Below is the mystery as recorded in (Psalms 100: 4).

> *Enter into his gates with thanksgiving, and into his courts with praise: be thankful unto him, and bless his name.*
>
> (Psalm 100:4).

The word courts used in the above scripture means His residence. The English dictionary gives the meaning of courts as *"sovereign's residence and retinue."* The scripture above shows us that through thanksgiving we can enter into the gates of the Most High but through praise can we access His courts or His residence and His entourage of angels.

When God's people begin to praise His Name, it sends the enemy running! I challenge you to become a person of praise, and you will experience the release of the Power of God. The Bible declares that God inhabits in the praises of His people (Psalm 22:3). In other words, God "dwells" in the atmosphere of praise. This means that praise is not the reaction of coming into His presence but the vehicle of faith that brings us into the presence and power of God! Praise is the doorway in the very sacredness of the glory of God.

The Psalmist as recorded in the scripture above admonishes us to enter His gates with thanksgiving, and His courts with praise. Praise brings our spirit into a pinnacle of fellowship and intimacy with God. It magnifies our awareness of our spiritual union with the Most High God. Praise transports us into the realm of the supernatural and into the glorious power of God.

> *"Blessed is the people that know the joyful sound: they shall walk, O LORD, in the light of thy countenance."*
>
> (Psalm 89:15).

The people that know the joyful sound of praise shall walk into the glorious presence or countenance of the Most High God the scripture declares.

Priests Functioning under the Glory

Priests can function under the glorious presence of God through praise and worship. Praise takes us into the very Cole of the presence of the presence of God and worship gives us a place to settle in the courts of the most High. You will most priests in their healing meetings will just be praising God. They would sing praises to the Lord and they sense that they've entered into the courts will start worshipping. At this point heaven and earth have connect and the throne of God the most High has descended and settled in the praise and worship. This is the time when all things become possible because the reality of Heaven has manifested in that particular meeting. If its pastor Benny Hinn he who at this point start telling people to do what they couldn't do before. This is because he knows that heaven has manifested death and all its friends from the pit of hell dethroned. When heaven manifests all people need is faith to receive what they believed God for. That the reason why pastor Benny Hinn would tell people to do what they could not do before. Just act in faith he says! I know you could not do it naturally but now you can do it if you just act in faith!

In another priest's ministry David Herzog, when heaven manifest in the Glory, great things happen, people receive gold teeth, people loose weight supernaturally, instantly! People receive money and many blessings when they sow in the glory. When the glory of God manifests death and all its friends; stress, sadness, poverty, disease, sickness etc disappears. They are dethroned from their place of authority. In the glory if you only act in faith the cause of the poverty, stress and death will be eliminated.

Kings Functioning under the Glory

Kings like priests enter the presence of God through praises and also find their place of rest in His courts through worship. When the glory of God really manifests in the assemblage kings receive Words for the people from the presence of God. These words are called words of knowledge and words of wisdom.

While the priests would tell people to do what they cannot do naturally, kings will receive words of knowledge concerning peoples' situations. Kings would go like so and so have a tumor in his brain and the Lord is healing that; so and so you've been on a wheel chair for so many years because of the accident you suffered, the Lord is healing that.

Pastor Chris as a king would go like; the presence of God to heal is in this place start receiving your healing. Sometimes he would generalize he would go like I rebuke cancer, HIV, paralysis and so on. The disease, sickness and whatever infirmity would respond to the Words of power in the presence of the Lord.

Kings also like Prophet T.B Joshua use a lot of words of wisdom. He would tell you your whole situation supernaturally and finally administer healing in the presence of the Glory of God. Kings unlike priests use words in the presence of God to dethrone death and its friends.

Paul and Silas in the Glory

And at midnight Paul and Silas prayed, and sang praises unto God: and the prisoners heard them. And suddenly there was a great earthquake, so that the foundations of the prison were shaken: and immediately all the doors were opened, and every one's bands were loosed

(Acts 16:25-26).

When Paul and Silas were arrested and put in prison. They immediately prayed and started praising God. As we discussed earlier, about praising being the doorway to the Glory. When Paul and Silas praised God the glory of the highest God descended on that prison. The effects were that the prison was hit by a great by a great earthquake. The place trembled at the coming of the Glory of God such that the foundations of the whole prison were opened. Because there is no dead situation in the Glory, no bondage or captivity in the glory realm, the chains were broken and the doors opened.

Notice this, the earthquake only hit the prison and no place else. This is because the glory only descended on the prison by the power of praise. He inhabits, dwells, is attracted by the praises of His children.

Then he called for a light, and sprang in, and came trembling, and fell down before Paul and Silas, And brought them out, and said, Sirs, what must I do to be saved?

(Acts 16:29-30).

The astounding things that happen in the Glory realm causes men acknowledge how much they need a salvation. When the glory realm manifests, wonders happen. These wonders make men to realize how inadequate they are. The result of this is the call for salvation. In the above scripture you will realize that the prison keeper was moved by the events that happened and also by the love shown to him by Paul. The result was "Sirs what must I do to be saved?"

When the glory of God manifest in an area, supernatural occurrences take place. In this case it was an earthquake but in other places different supernatural things happen. I remember one time back in Zambia I was praising and praying in tongues with my friends. This time I had just been baptized in the Holy Ghost and I was very excited about speaking in tongues. When praise went deep and deep, I started loosing my earthly conscious. I was kind of like transported to a different realm where I heard people worshipping God in spiritually deep and intimate way. At this point I started disconnecting deliberately because I wanted to find out who is singing. When I looked everyone was praying. I was surprised as I heard the singing even louder and more clearly. Then I realized that I've entered another realm of operations. I started saying "I can hear the angels singing!" this dropped even deeper into this realm such that I didn't know when the meeting ended. The next thing I felt was people carrying me.

He Shows Deep Things in the Glory Realm

The Lord shows great and deep things in the glory realm. He has on several occasions taken to places and made me experience things so astounding in the realm of the Glory. One of the occasions I do not know where I was dreaming on not, where I was in the flesh or in spirit. the Lord took me to a place which has streets of Gold. This place was like the high way. The road was made out of Gold and there was green grass very well cut on the sides of the road. The road was very long and there was a very white light ahead of the road. I couldn't see where the road was going because the light was too bright. The highway has gold street lights. There was no one else on the road apart from me and the instructor whom I cannot tell because I just could hear His voice. The feeling was that He was behind me but I still couldn't see His face for whatever reasons.

The more recent experience of what I could term the glorious realm was very vivid as well, even more vivid than the past experiences.

This time around, again I couldn't tell whether I was sleeping or not. I couldn't tell whether I was in the flesh on in the spirit. This time I saw an old, old man. This man was floating in the clouds and a great wind was blowing on Him. He had long grey hair which moving as a result of the wind. He was dressed in a purple garment. Something which looks like a royal garment, he was dressed like royalty, like a King. He was looking very fresh on His face. He is old but he wasn't wrinkled on His face. He didn't show any signs of stress or weakness due to old age. He looked old but young. He had this innocence on His face, He looked old but had the countenance of a baby. I don't exactly know how I can describe this old man. He is still a wonder today as He was the day or night I saw Him. This old man was smiling at me. The more He smiled the more loved I felt. I felt so overwhelmed by His love; the intensity of His love was so strong such that I started squeezing myself. I really felt helpless, because I felt there is nothing I can do to replicate this love. I realized that the kind and intensity of this love is beyond my capacity to both comprehend and replicate. This experience changed my life; it altered my understanding of the love for God. He loves us so much so that nothing can we do to replicate His love for us. When I think of this experience I get paralyzed in my system. It always makes me felt humbled and privileged to be loved that way. I don't really know who that old man is but the first thoughts that came to my mind were I have seen the ancient of days!

In august of 2010, we had a 10day prayer and fasting. This prayer and fasting is like nothing I have seen or experienced before. It was so full of the anointing of the Holy Ghost and so full of the glory of God. I remember day 7 of the prayer and fasting. As I was praying moving back and forth, I saw something in the other room. There was nothing in that room but I felt like I saw something. I brushed it off and I passed by the same door I saw it again. This time around I paused a bit from my praying and looked around the room. There was still nothing in the room but a very unusually thick presence of God. I was startled but went back to praying. The third time as a passed by the same door I saw something like a human being again. At the same time I heard a voice saying there are angels in this room. At that very moment I stopped praying. Asked everyone to stop praying and said to them "Do you know that there are angles in this room?" I went on to say if you want to experience the glorious presence of go in. the guys were very skeptical then one lady went in. the moment she entered she was slain and was down for some time. Then she started crying and crying. I got concerned, went in and pulled her out of the room. When she got back to herself I asked her what happened. Then she told us that the angle of the Lord took her by the hand and showed her, her family. The family was all in a queue heading towards a great deep fuming with fire. She said she also saw some of her relatives including her late mother burning in the fire in the great deep. She saw her family members who are currently alive on the queue towards destruction and the sick cousin just about to drop into the deep of fire. This and many other things did the Lord show us in the glory realm when we had a 10day prayer and fasting.

Declaring the Kingdom of Heaven

And as ye go, preach, saying, The kingdom of heaven is at hand. Heal the sick, cleanse the lepers, raise the dead, cast out devils: freely ye have received, freely give.

(Matthew 10:7-8).

The whole essence of Kingdom is rulership as explained in the earlier chapters of the book. Therefore if the Kingdom of Heaven is declared with understanding the will or rulership of heaven descends. The Lord Jesus when teaching His disciples to pray declared; "thy will be done on earth as it is in heaven." This is exactly what happens when the kingdom of heaven is declared. The will of God in heaven takes effect on earth.

In the opening scripture the Lord admonished His disciples to go and PREACH, PROCLAIM, DECLARE! Saying the Kingdom of Heaven is at hand. The instruction was to declare that the kingdom of heaven is at hand. When the Kingdom of Heaven is declared in faith the will of God in heaven comes to earth. This effectively means the glory of God in heaven descends. He admonished them to heal the sick, cleanse the lepers, raise the dead and to cast out devils after preaching the Kingdom of heaven is at hand.

The Lord gave this order of preaching the Kingdom of heaven first then healing the sick. This is because He understood that in heaven there is no death and all its friends. So He taught them to say if you only invite heaven in your meeting you can heal the sick, cleans the lepers and raise the dead. This is because when heaven descends in a place death and all its friends are dethroned from their strong standing.

When the Kingdom of Heaven is effectively declared in faith, the glory of the heavens descends. The will of God in heaven is extended to the particular place when heaven is being declared. The astounding things Apostle Paul saw in the heavens become realities in that particular place. Declaring the Kingdom of Heaven brings the heavenly hosts to your meetings. The glory of the throne of God becomes a reality in your assemblage.

Wisdom of Performing Miracles using Exousia

This is the wisdom of performing miracles using the Word of God. Exousia is the authority in the Word. Because the Word is one of the authorities in heaven besides the Father and the Holy Spirit it has the power and wisdom to do miracles, signs and wonders. *"And he said unto them, Go ye into all the world, and preach the gospel to every creature. He that believeth and is baptized shall be saved; but he that believeth not shall be damned. And these signs shall follow them that BELIEVE; In my name shall they cast out devils; ....; .... they shall lay hands on the sick, and they shall recover." (Luke 16:15-18).*

The mystery behind performing miracles using the Word of God is in believing. The scripture above declares that those who receive and believe the gospel shall cast out devils and lay hands on the sick and the sick shall be healed. If you believe what the Bible says and put it to work you access the power or authority of the Word to perform miracles.

The integrity of God is in His Word. So He cannot go against His Word. If He says it, He will perform it according as He has said. The Lords' eyes are looking constantly on His Word to perform it *(Jeremiah 1:12).*

If the Word says you shall lay hands on the sick and the sick shall be healed, and you believe that Word in your heart. When you lay hands on the sick they shall be healed.

I know of one evangelist who functioned so much in the realm of Exousia. Evangelist, Earnest Angley. This man did not perform miracles using some anointing (Dunamis) or under the glory. He just believed the Word and laid his hands on the sick and the sick were healed.

And the prayer of faith shall save the sick, and the Lord shall raise him up; and if he have committed sins, they shall be forgiven him.

(James 5:15).

Faith is putting to practice what you believe in the Word of God. The scripture above says a prayer that comes from believing the Word of God shall heal the sick and cover multitudes of sins. Faith is not based on the Holy Spirit but on the Word of God.

The cornerstone for performing miracles using exousia the authority of the Word of God is faith. Faith in what the Word says produces the authority of the Word to thwart devils, poison, disease and sickness.

Declaring the Kingdom of God

In March 2009, we had a conference in Kabwata, Lusaka Zambia. We did all we had to do, we paid for the venue distributed the flyers and put all the advertising both on Radio Christian Voice and banners in town, Kabwata and the neighbouring places. All was set and all was well. We prayed for the conference and everything was happening well. On the day of the Conference the other church, which is renting the same premise suddenly, came up with a programme. Confusion started, my assistant, pastor Kelvin was a little more upset because he was surprised at their behavior then he called upon me to address the situation. I was busy organizing other things concerning the same event, and then I remembered that I have EXOUSIA in the Kingdom of God. I immediately started declaring the Kingdom of God on the confusion; I did that as many times as I could. When I arrived at the place I requested audience with the senior pastor of the same church, to my surprise the man was humbled at talking with me, the man changed suddenly and started offering things to me. He offered me all their musical instruments and the people to play the instruments, he gave us the hall well decorated, they did everything for us, and all we did was to put a few flowers on the pulpit. He even offered a set of music instruments for us to use each time we have an event of that nature.

The Authority of the Kingdom of God; …..the authority of the Word of God; the Authority of Kings, "EXOUSIA" Glory to God. Just declare the Kingdom of God when dealing with a clash on authority.

The Wisdom of Performing Miracles using Dunamis

The wisdom of performing miracles using Dunamis is the mystery of doing wondrous things by the power of the Holy Spirit. This is the wisdom of doing the astounding things by the third establishment or authority in heaven the Holy Spirit. The power or anointing of the Holy Spirit comes in form of a blanket covering upon you. it has occurred to me several times when I a heavy blanket like covering upon me then I'll be moved to lay hands, blow on the sick. at times even I'd receive words of knowledge for particular people in the assemblage. One thing I have noticed in the operation of the Dunamis is that He responds to the word of God. Whenever am teaching on some topic the blanket like covering usually covers me. This covering sometimes gives me a supernatural ability to explain the word of God *(John 14:26).* He is always present to fulfill what I am teaching about. He comes to give effect to the words I speak. I have noticed that I don't usually need praise and worship for Him to manifest His power. Sometimes I would be busy with other things, but when am asked to pray for someone He would immediately envelope me with same presence. His major job description is to give effect to the Word of God *(John 15:26).* When am teaching on the Glory of God, He manifests the Glory of God; when am teaching on healing, He manifests healing. When am teaching on the power of the Word of God, He manifests the power of the Word *(John 16:14).* He is the one who gives effect to the Word of God.

There is wisdom in the effective working in the Power of the Holy Spirit. One has to understand certain principles in order to effectively function in the power of the Holy Spirit. Below are some of the principles of functioning with Dunamis:

* **Yielding to the direction of the Holy Spirit (No hard and fast rule):**

Many in the body of Christ today think there is a hard and fast rule to functioning in the power of the Holy Spirit. Many are lead to believe that if you pray and fast more, you will perform more miracles. This is not so, all you have to do is to learn to make the Holy Spirit your master. You need to learn to be weak and to yield yourself to the Spirit.

Many believers want to function the same way as pastor "GREAT" is doing it. So they think if I act this way, do my hands like this and then talk like this, I will get the Holy Spirit do what I want since that's how pastor "GREAT" does it and he gets results. This is so wrong; there is no formula for working miracles. Yield to the Spirit and he will lead you.

In august of 2010 we had a time of prayer and fasting, during that time a certain women in her late 50s came for the meeting. This women was an intercessor from a local church, she was looking so confused, sad and depressed. As the meeting went on I asked her what was wrong. Then she narrated that as she was interceding with her friends at a camp meeting, she saw a skeleton approaching towards her, then when she opened her eyes to see there was nothing. All the sudden she felt like someone was coming from behind her. After this she got drowse and fainted, from that moment on she got confused and sometimes had relapses and loose her mind. When she finished telling me what happened, I got numb, I didn't know what to do with her, then the Spirit in his power lead me to stand behind her, I stood behind her and she immediately fell by the power of the Holy Spirit. When she got up, she was completely healed. She testified that as I stood behind her she felt like I was sucking something from her brain.

Glory to God! This is how it works; I could have easily used my experience and pray but I chose to yield to the Spirit and she was delivered within seconds.

- **Be full of the Word of God.**

The Holy Spirit responds to the Word. He does not testify of Himself. He testifies of Jesus who is the Word of God. The more the Word of God is working in your life, the more freedom the Holy Spirit will have in your life to operate. He can only function with the amount of the Word of God you've become. Jesus Christ became 100% the Word of God and it was said of Him that He had the Spirit without measure. The Word of God is not meant for head knowledge, it is meant to transform us into its Image. Reading the Word of God gives us knowledge about the Word, but studying it makes us become like the Word of God who is Christ Jesus our Lord.

- **Acknowledging the Holy Spirit as your partner:**

There is a great always a great connection in the scriptures between performing miracles and the power of the Holy Spirit. on a number of times you hear in the scripture that so and so moved in the power of the Holy Spirit and did great things. Lets look at the statement by Christ Jesus in Luke 4:18.

"The Spirit of the Lord is upon me, because he hath anointed me to preach the gospel to the poor; he hath sent me to heal the brokenhearted, to preach deliverance to the captives, and recovering of sight to the blind, to set at liberty them that are bruised."

Here in the scripture above the Lord Jesus acknowledge the partnership between Him and the Holy Spirit. The Lord Jesus didn't say the Spirit of the Lord Has preached the gospel to the poor; he has healed the brokenhearted and preached deliverance to the captives. Etc. in other word the Lord Jesus said the Spirit of the Lord has given me the ability to preach the gospel to the poor; he has given the ability to heal the broken hearted and so on.

The same way the Lord Jesus partnered with the Holy Spirit and acknowledged the partnership. We have to partner and acknowledge the partnership with the Holy Spirit to do wonderful works. Let's look at another example of how another apostle acknowledged the partnership between the Lord Jesus and the Holy Spirit.

> *"How God anointed Jesus of Nazareth with the Holy Ghost and with power: who went about doing good, and healing all that were oppressed of the devil; for God was with him."*
>
> (Acts 10:38).

God anointed Jesus Christ with the Holy Ghost and with power. Then Jesus with the partnership of the anointing and the power of the Holy Ghost went about doing good, and healing all that were oppressed of the devil. Then the verse ends with for God (the Holy Ghost) was with Him. A big note to remember is that Jesus functioned like you and I here on earth as a son of man.

- **Dunamis the power for ministry:**

Many believers out of ignorance have limited the power of the Holy Spirit to some olive oil in a bottle called the anointing oil. This truly one of the ways this power can be stored but by far not the only way. The power of the Holy Spirit, the Dunamis is primarily the power for ministry. The Bible says that you shall receive power after that the Holy come upon you. this power is for you to be witnesses of His to the rest of the world. *"But ye shall receive power, after that the Holy Ghost is come upon you: and ye shall be WITNESSES unto me both in Jerusalem, and in all Judaea, and in Samaria, and unto the uttermost part of the earth." (Acts 1:8).*

The scripture emphasizes the fact that you shall receive power (Dunamis) to be my witnesses after that the Holy Spirit has come upon you. The Holy Spirit gives us Dunamis for ministry; to minister with boldness. This power is not given for the purposes of showing the world that you are anointed. It is given as a tool to help you do the work He has called you to do. The Spirit through Dunamis gives us the power to bring heaven in every place we find ourselves. We have power to bring peace and love in every place we go. Let Dunamis reign in you, let power reign in you, let heaven reign in you!

Falling Under the Power of the Holy Spirit

Dunamis short-circuits your strength to work well in you. Just like when a stronger currency of electricity is allowed to flow through a system, which is weaker, a short circuit occurs. The same happens with us, when the stronger currency of the Holy Spirit the Dunamis flows through our weaker systems, our systems short circuit and fails. This gives way to the stronger currency of the Holy Spirit in our lives. This is the reason why people fall when the Holy Spirit descends on them; their strengths are short-circuited and fail.

The scripture declares that his strength is made perfect in our weakness, so for his strength to be perfect in you, your strength has to weaken. Whenever your strength fails, his strength the Dunamis is at best. Falling results from the short-circuiting of your strength, at this point is when the Spirit is at his strongest working on all your needy areas.

There are times when the church is worshipping miracles start happening, this is because the dunamis has brought heaven on earth. Other times you find the pastor blowing on a sick person and the person gets healed, that's the dunamis at work.

I have experienced the way dunamis works a couple of times in my ministry. I don't really decide to do some things I do, but rather am lead by the Holy Spirit to do them. Sometimes the Holy Spirit leads me to blowing on some people and they are healed, others times He leads me to just touch the place that is in pain and the pain could go at once. Other times I use a word of Knowledge and the sickness and pain goes at once.

There was one time during my LXP year; I had a very troubling situation. This situation was mostly doctrinal because it had something to do with falling under the Dunamis the power of the Holy Ghost. It so happened that during one of the meetings as I was praying for the people, they started falling under the power of the Holy Spirit. This brought a lot questions as to how of all people do I manage to make people fall? There was this particular time we were at one of the Disciples of God meetings, this time like everyone else I started to pray for the boys and girls. On that day every person I prayed for could fall under the power of the Holy Ghost. This brought a lot of sceptism, in the team. There was a lot of talking among the staff and my fellow students, whereby some started say that am pushing and tripping the people I pray for. This troubled for the whole time, such that I resorted to taking the matter to the Lord in prayer. In specific I asked the Lord to vindicate me, to prove that it wasn't my doing but the work of the power of the Holy Spirit. In answer to that the Lord showed me in a dream that He will give me a chance to prove that it's the Holy Spirit. After that dream, I started in my own ways trying to create ways of demonstrating the power of the Holy Spirit. "I said to myself I will ask for 5 minutes after lessons to demonstrate the power of the Holy Spirit." Each time I tried and I couldn't get the 5 minute to do my demonstrations and vindicate myself as shown in a dream. Then one day, one of the Leaders came to me, and asked me to explain to the Disciples of God, why they fall when I pray for them. Immediately I realized that what the Lord showed me would happen, and I told my leader that the Lord revealed to me in a dream that this will happen. The brother went on to say that before I can be given chance to talk to the D.O.Gs I first had to tell the team of my fellow students and the Leaders what I was going to say to the D.O.Gs for approval. But I knew what I had to do according as I was given in a dream; I was supposed to demonstrate the power of the Holy Spirit with my fellow students.

With this in mind, I just said a few things and asked three guys to come to the front. I told them that I will not lay hands on these people but they will fall under the power of the Holy Spirit. I even went on to say I will just count up to 9 and each of these will fall under the power of the Spirit. I asked 3 guys and made them stand about 2.5metres away from me. Then I started, I counted the first 3, for the father, the son and the Holy Spirit and the first one fail under the power of the Spirit; then I went on and counted the next 3, and the second one fail under the power of the Holy Spirit; and then the third one fail.

I believe there is no rule to how the Spirit works it's just yielding to the move and getting along.

Inviting Musa George Mwanza
to your area

Musa George Mwanza may be available to speak at your church, conference, or crusade. Please contact us with the details of your ministry and your invitation. You must also give information of the nature of the event. Musa and his team will pray over your invitation and respond to you as soon as possible.

E-mail: musagmwanza@gmail.com

Tongues of Angels Unveiled

Tongues of Angels Unveiled explores this Spiritual exercise of speaking in tongues with so much depth that it rediscovers, reveals and unveils all the 5 different kinds of tongues and their respective significances, to believers and the body of Christ. This book will not only reveal to you the power and purpose of each of the 5 different kind of tongues but it will also take you through a process of discovering this spiritual gift as it answers most of the questions you may have about speaking in tongues.

God's Medicine Bottle for Sin and Addictions

The Medicine Bottle is a step by step answer to problems of addictive sinful practices, it comprises of grace pills, days of fasting and confessional prayers to help you walk out of your sinful habits and tendencies.

Grace Pills

Grace Pill for Addictive Habits
Addictive habits? Go for the pill and you will find rest. Condemnation is the greatest weapon the enemy uses to keep you in bondage. Are you struggling with something? Do not condemn yourself, do not feel condemned because Jesus does not condemn you!
There is no condemnation for those that are in Christ!
And the Grace is sufficient for your struggle, go for the pill and you will find rest! Our struggles are the reason why Jesus died for us on the cross! Don't be ashamed of your struggles, be free to share and make known your mistakes. Grace is only sufficient for the wrong we do.
Weakness is mankind's greatest gift! Why are we ashamed of being wrong? Why are we afraid of being weak?
Go for pill and find rest!!